DYNAMITE ENTERTAINMENT PROUDLY PRESENTS

CHARLAINE HARRIS
GRAVE SIGHT™
BOOK TWO

DYNAMITE ENTERTAINMENT PROUDLY PRESENTS

CHARLAINE HARRIS
GRAVE SIGHT
BOOK TWO

written by CHARLAINE HARRIS & WILLIAM HARMS
art by DENIS MEDRI
colors by PAOLO FRANCESCUTTO Gotem Studio
letters by BILL TORTOLINI
cover by BENOIT SPRINGER

contributing editor RICH YOUNG
consultation ERNST DABEL & LES DABEL
special thanks to JOSHUA BILMES

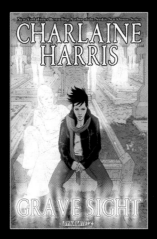

ISBN10: 1-60690-239-3
ISBN13: 978-1-60690-239-4

10 9 8 7 6 5 4 3 2

Dynamite Entertainment:

NICK BARRUCCI · PRESIDENT
JUAN COLLADO · CHIEF OPERATING OFFICER
JOSEPH RYBANDT · EDITOR
JOSH JOHNSON · CREATIVE DIRECTOR
RICH YOUNG · BUSINESS DEVELOPMENT
JASON ULLMEYER · SENIOR DESIGNER
JOSH JOHNSON · TRAFFIC COORDINATOR
CHRIS CANIANO · PRODUCTION ASSISTANT

WWW.DYNAMITE.NET

For media rights, foreign rights, promotions, licensing, and advertising: marketing@dynamite.net

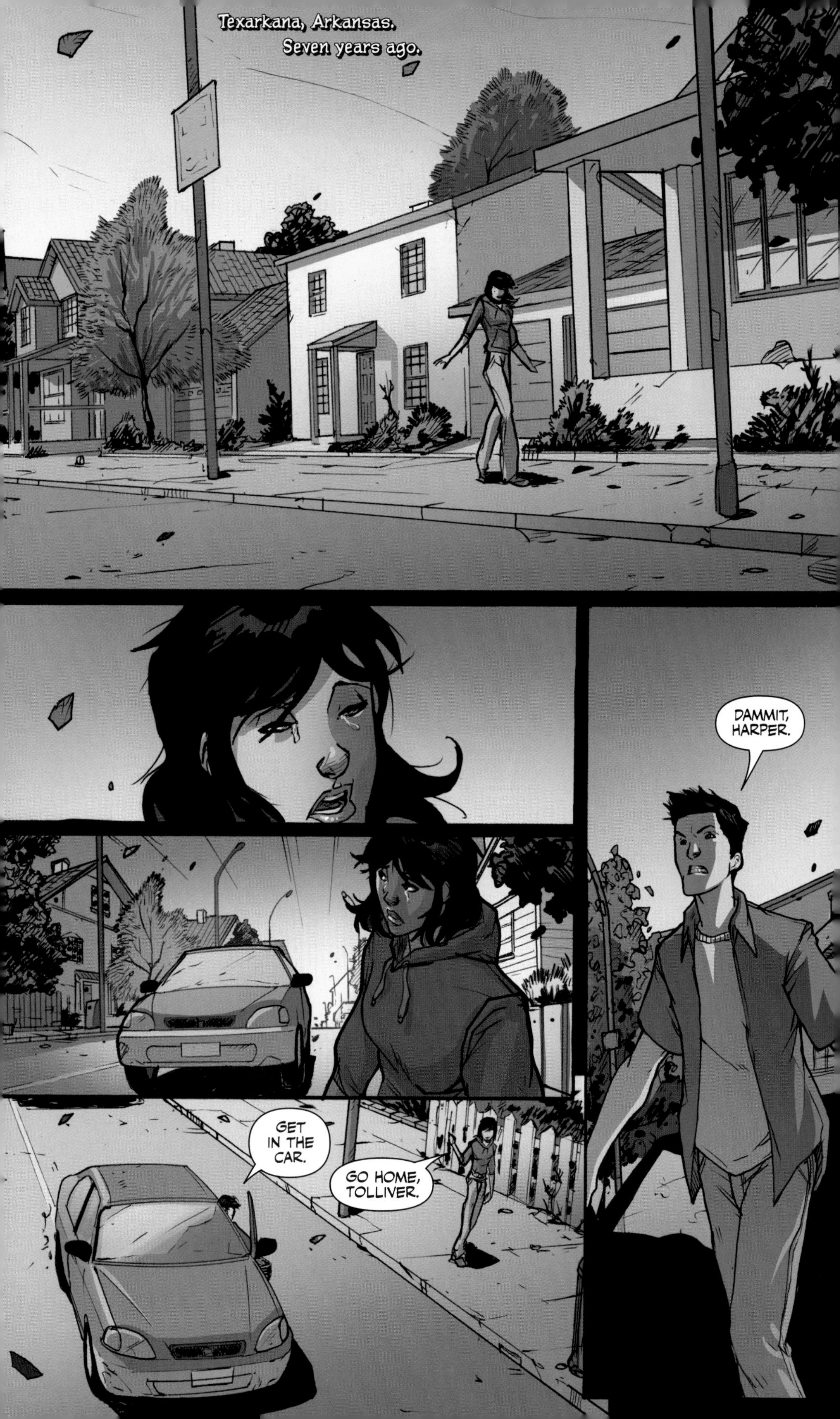
Texarkana, Arkansas.
Seven years ago.
DAMMIT, HARPER.
GET IN THE CAR.
GO HOME, TOLLIVER.

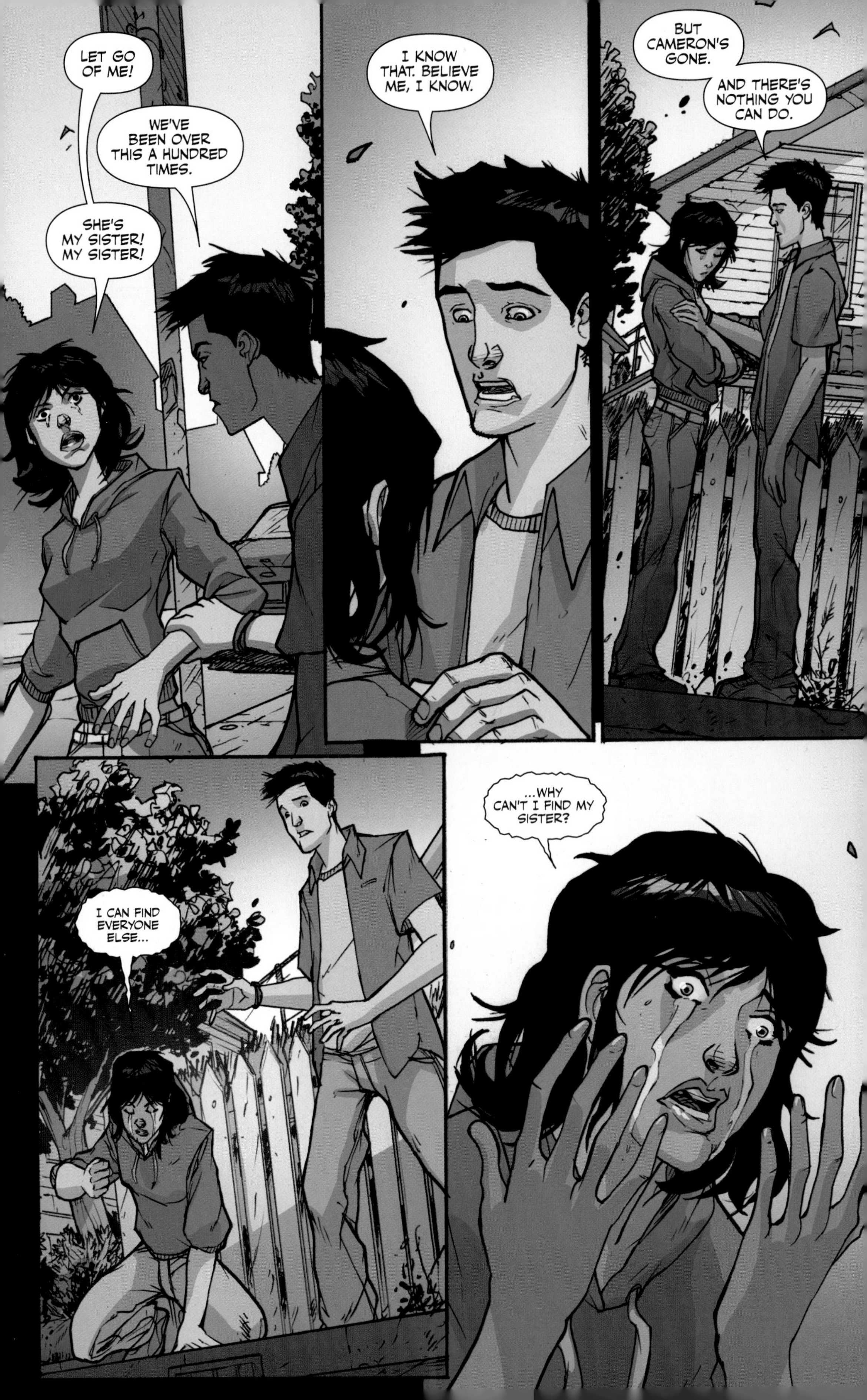
LET GO OF ME!
WE'VE BEEN OVER THIS A HUNDRED TIMES.
SHE'S MY SISTER! MY SISTER!
I KNOW THAT. BELIEVE ME, I KNOW.
BUT CAMERON'S GONE.
AND THERE'S NOTHING YOU CAN DO.
I CAN FIND EVERYONE ELSE...
...WHY CAN'T I FIND MY SISTER?

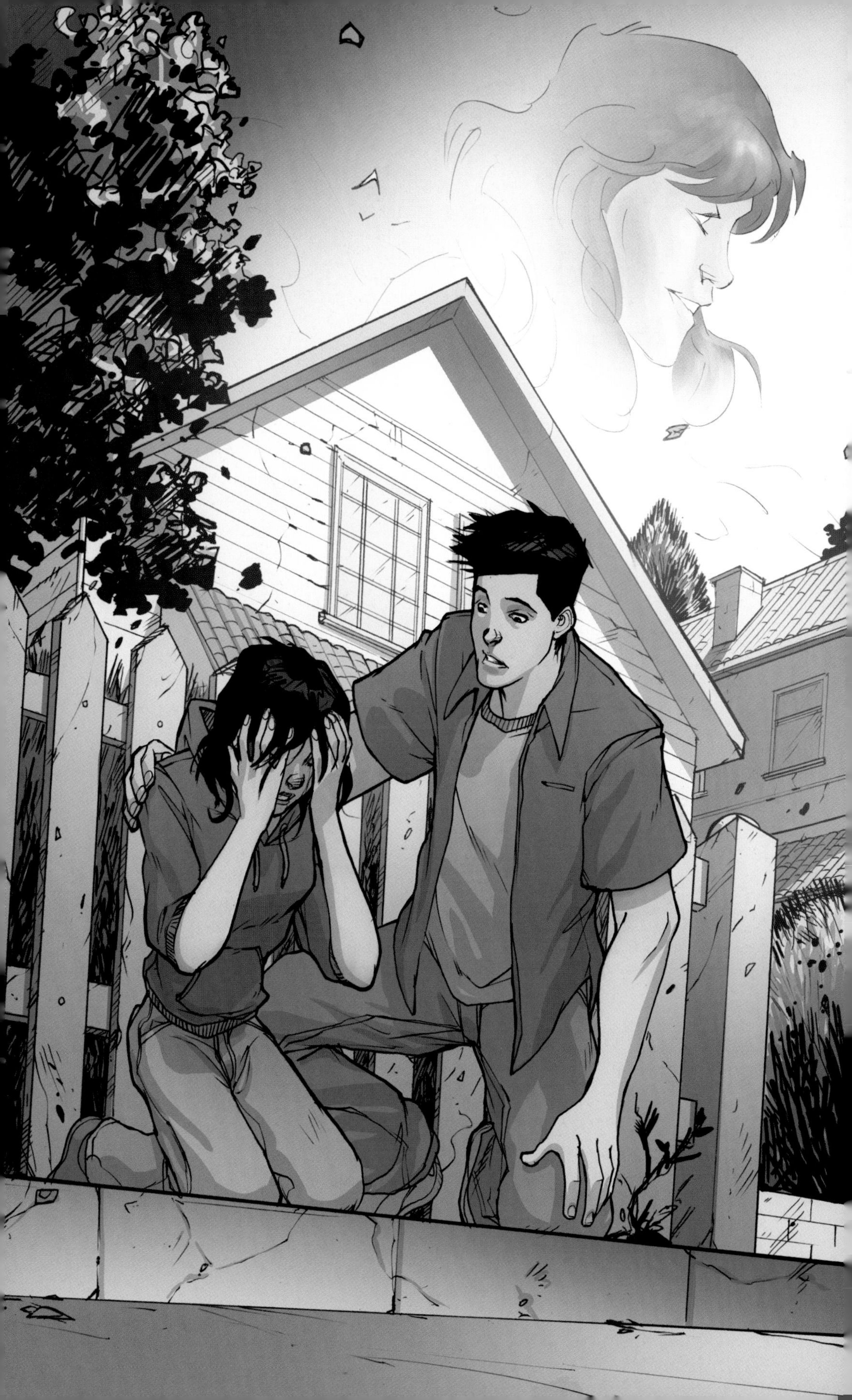

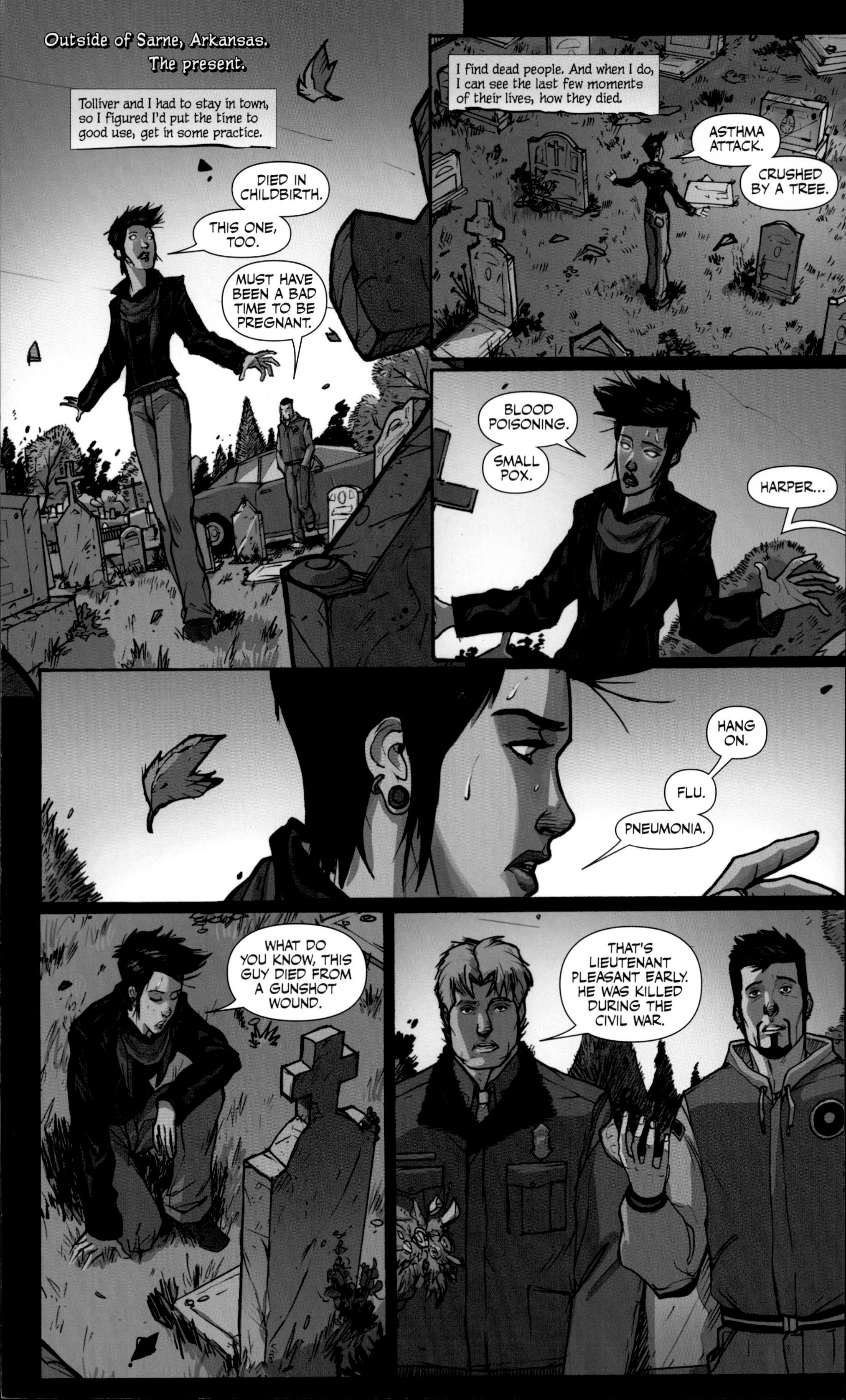
Outside of Sarne, Arkansas.
The present.
Tolliver and I had to stay in town, so I figured I'd put the time to good use, get in some practice.
DIED IN CHILDBIRTH.
THIS ONE, TOO.
MUST HAVE BEEN A BAD TIME TO BE PREGNANT.
I find dead people. And when I do, I can see the last few moments of their lives, how they died.
ASTHMA ATTACK.
CRUSHED BY A TREE.
BLOOD POISONING.
SMALL POX.
HARPER...
HANG ON.
FLU.
PNEUMONIA.
WHAT DO YOU KNOW, THIS GUY DIED FROM A GUNSHOT WOUND.
THAT'S LIEUTENANT PLEASANT EARLY. HE WAS KILLED DURING THE CIVIL WAR.

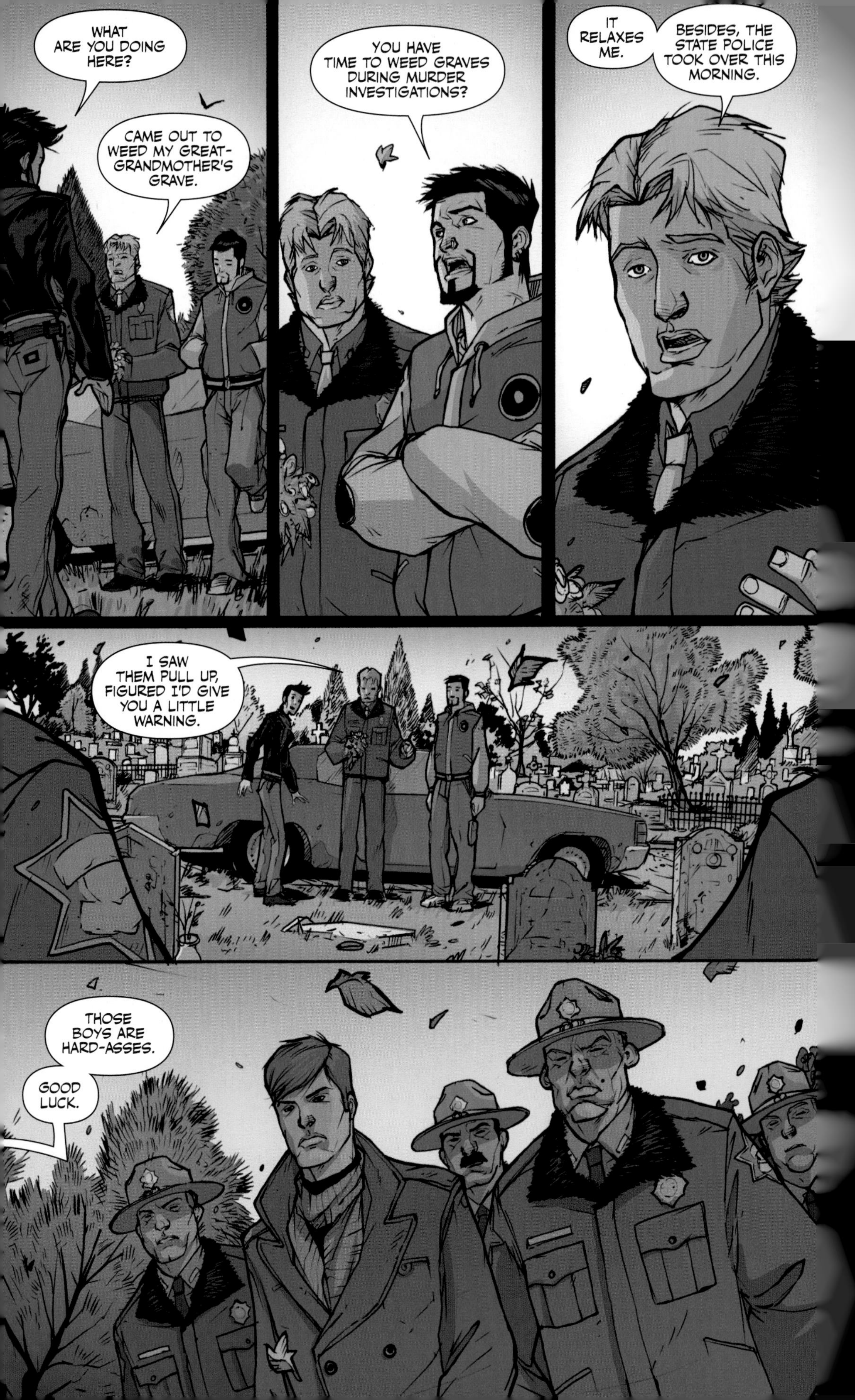
WHAT ARE YOU DOING HERE?
CAME OUT TO WEED MY GREAT-GRANDMOTHER'S GRAVE.
YOU HAVE TIME TO WEED GRAVES DURING MURDER INVESTIGATIONS?
IT RELAXES ME.
BESIDES, THE STATE POLICE TOOK OVER THIS MORNING.
I SAW THEM PULL UP, FIGURED I'D GIVE YOU A LITTLE WARNING.
THOSE BOYS ARE HARD-ASSES.
GOOD LUCK.

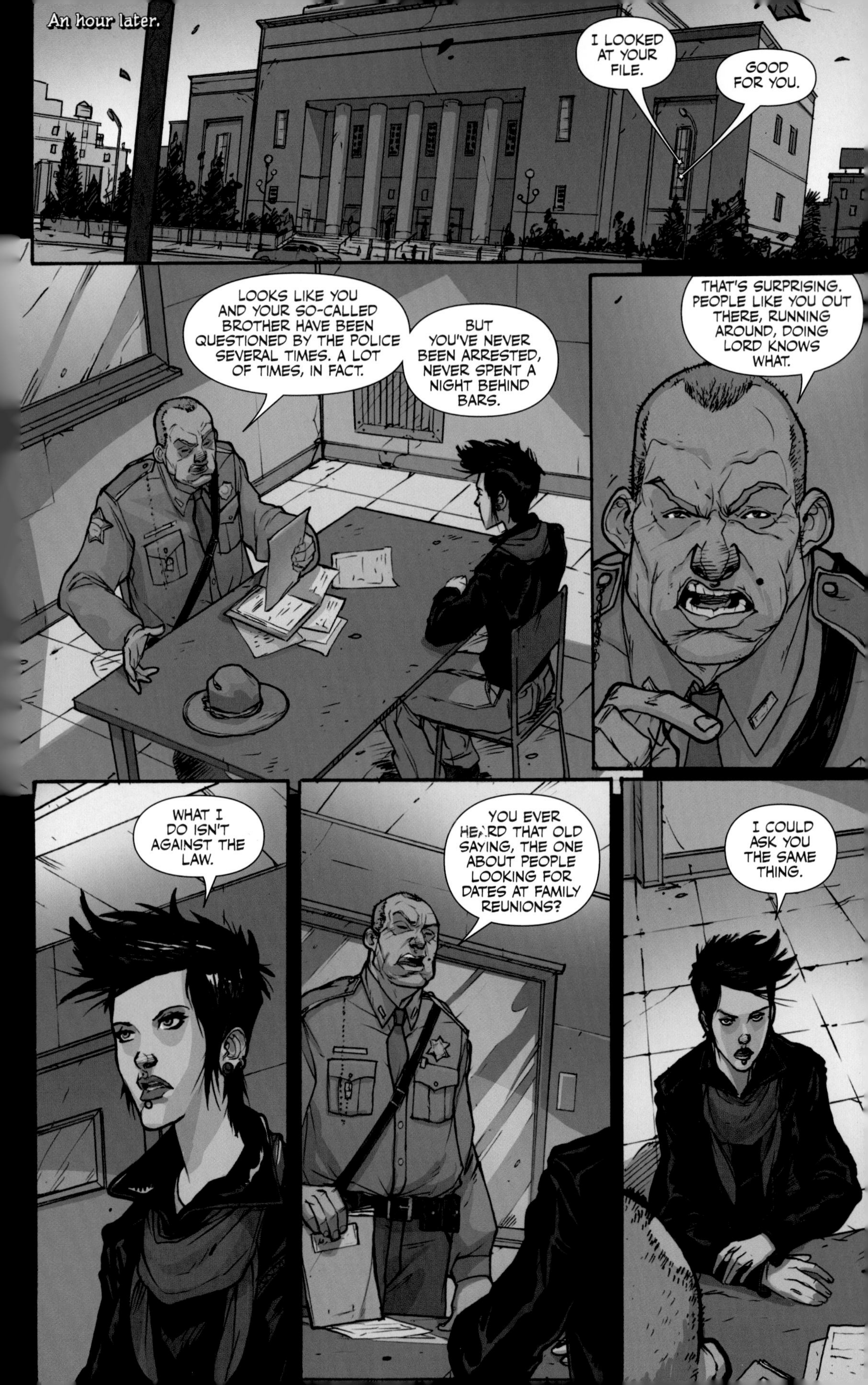
An hour later.
I LOOKED AT YOUR FILE.
GOOD FOR YOU.
LOOKS LIKE YOU AND YOUR SO-CALLED BROTHER HAVE BEEN QUESTIONED BY THE POLICE SEVERAL TIMES. A LOT OF TIMES, IN FACT.
BUT YOU'VE NEVER BEEN ARRESTED, NEVER SPENT A NIGHT BEHIND BARS.
THAT'S SURPRISING. PEOPLE LIKE YOU OUT THERE, RUNNING AROUND, DOING LORD KNOWS WHAT.
WHAT I DO ISN'T AGAINST THE LAW.
YOU EVER HEARD THAT OLD SAYING, THE ONE ABOUT PEOPLE LOOKING FOR DATES AT FAMILY REUNIONS?
I COULD ASK YOU THE SAME THING.

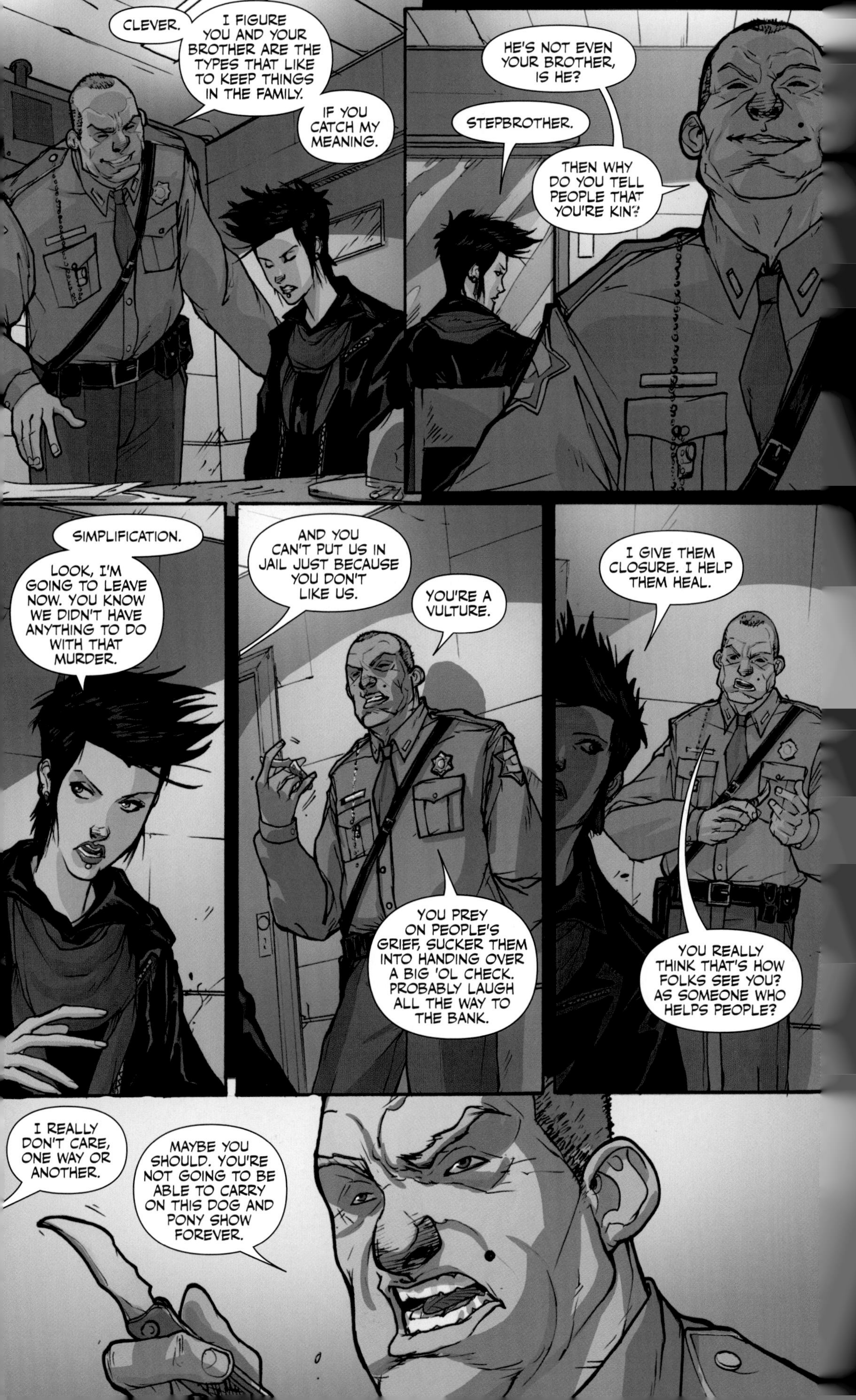
CLEVER.
I FIGURE YOU AND YOUR BROTHER ARE THE TYPES THAT LIKE TO KEEP THINGS IN THE FAMILY.
IF YOU CATCH MY MEANING.
HE'S NOT EVEN YOUR BROTHER, IS HE?
STEPBROTHER.
THEN WHY DO YOU TELL PEOPLE THAT YOU'RE KIN?
SIMPLIFICATION.
LOOK, I'M GOING TO LEAVE NOW. YOU KNOW WE DIDN'T HAVE ANYTHING TO DO WITH THAT MURDER.
AND YOU CAN'T PUT US IN JAIL JUST BECAUSE YOU DON'T LIKE US.
YOU'RE A VULTURE.
YOU PREY ON PEOPLE'S GRIEF, SUCKER THEM INTO HANDING OVER A BIG 'OL CHECK. PROBABLY LAUGH ALL THE WAY TO THE BANK.
I GIVE THEM CLOSURE. I HELP THEM HEAL.
YOU REALLY THINK THAT'S HOW FOLKS SEE YOU? AS SOMEONE WHO HELPS PEOPLE?
I REALLY DON'T CARE, ONE WAY OR ANOTHER.
MAYBE YOU SHOULD. YOU'RE NOT GOING TO BE ABLE TO CARRY ON THIS DOG AND PONY SHOW FOREVER.

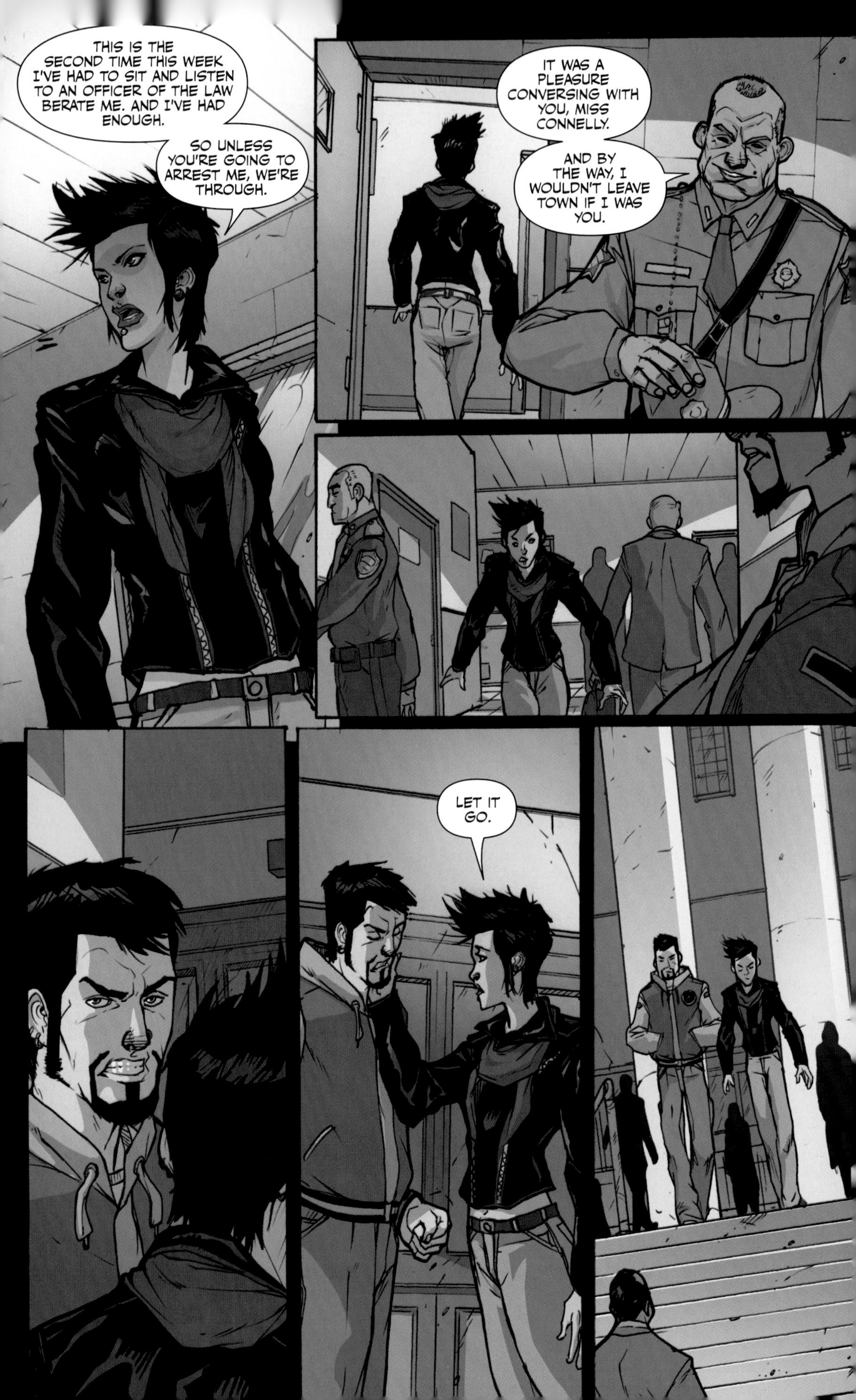
THIS IS THE SECOND TIME THIS WEEK I'VE HAD TO SIT AND LISTEN TO AN OFFICER OF THE LAW BERATE ME. AND I'VE HAD ENOUGH.
SO UNLESS YOU'RE GOING TO ARREST ME, WE'RE THROUGH.
IT WAS A PLEASURE CONVERSING WITH YOU, MISS CONNELLY.
AND BY THE WAY, I WOULDN'T LEAVE TOWN IF I WAS YOU.
LET IT GO.

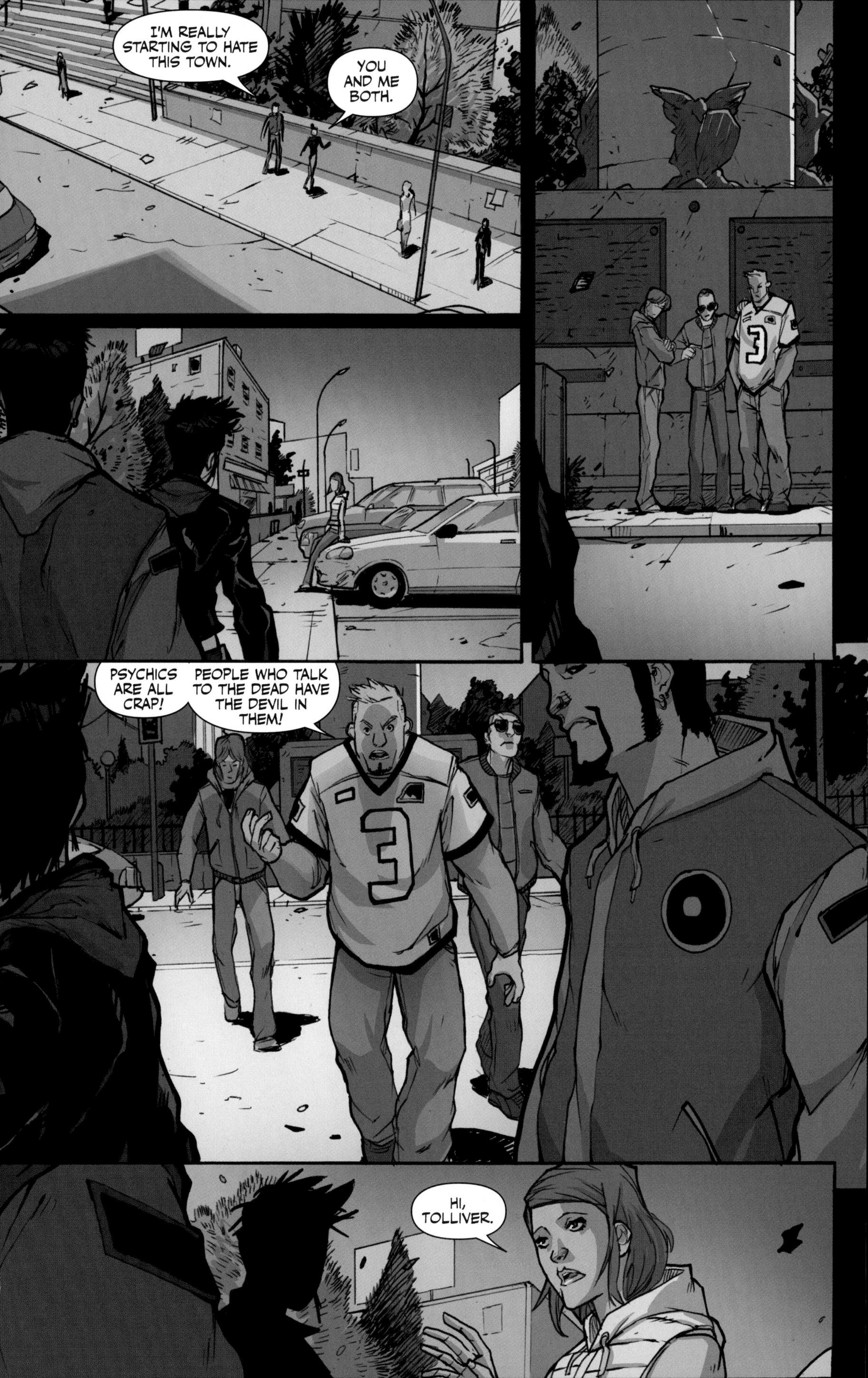
I'M REALLY STARTING TO HATE THIS TOWN.
YOU AND ME BOTH.
PSYCHICS ARE ALL CRAP!
PEOPLE WHO TALK TO THE DEAD HAVE THE DEVIL IN THEM!
HI, TOLLIVER.

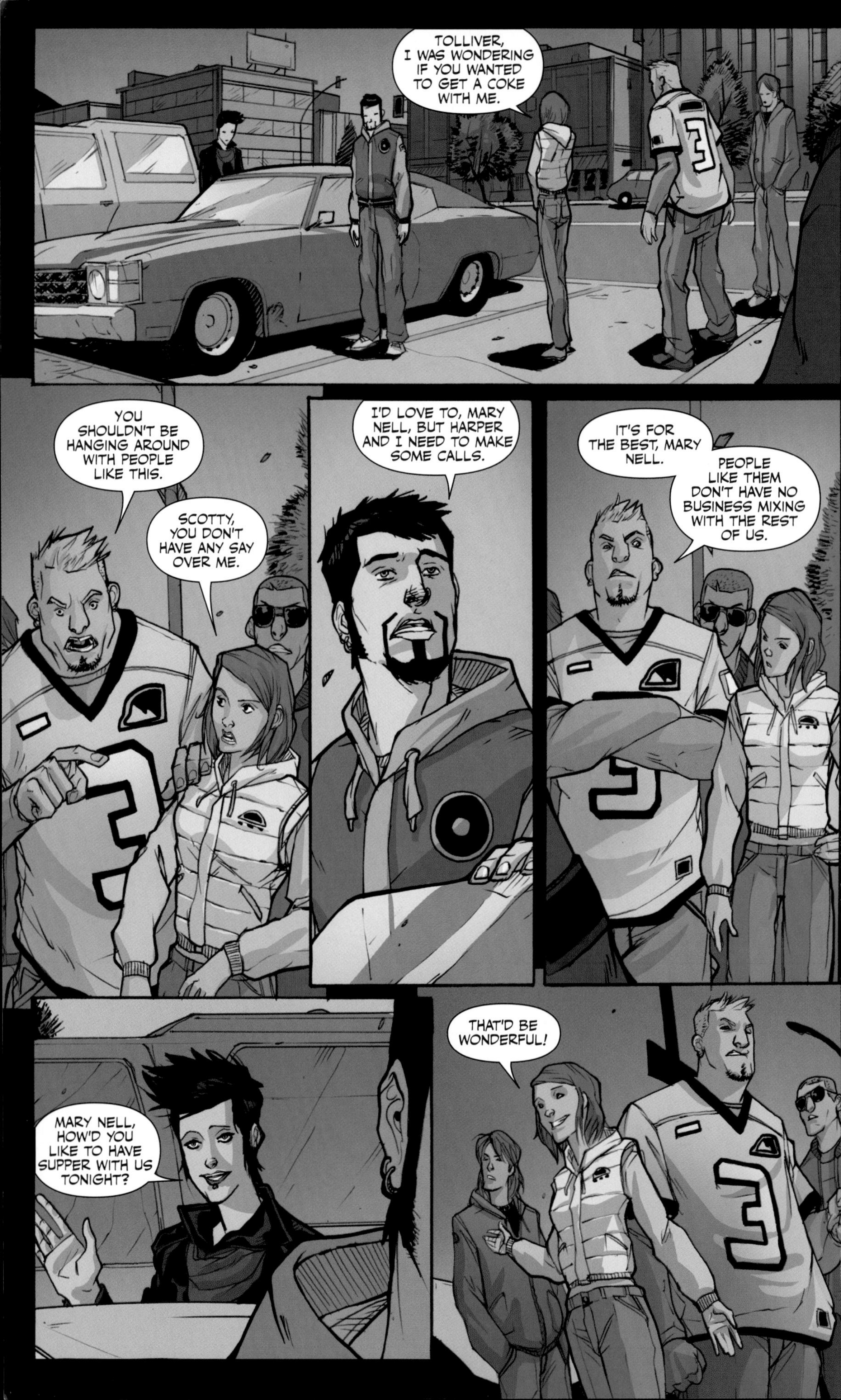
TOLLIVER, I WAS WONDERING IF YOU WANTED TO GET A COKE WITH ME.
YOU SHOULDN'T BE HANGING AROUND WITH PEOPLE LIKE THIS.
SCOTTY, YOU DON'T HAVE ANY SAY OVER ME.
I'D LOVE TO, MARY NELL, BUT HARPER AND I NEED TO MAKE SOME CALLS.
IT'S FOR THE BEST, MARY NELL.
PEOPLE LIKE THEM DON'T HAVE NO BUSINESS MIXING WITH THE REST OF US.
MARY NELL, HOW'D YOU LIKE TO HAVE SUPPER WITH US TONIGHT?
THAT'D BE WONDERFUL!

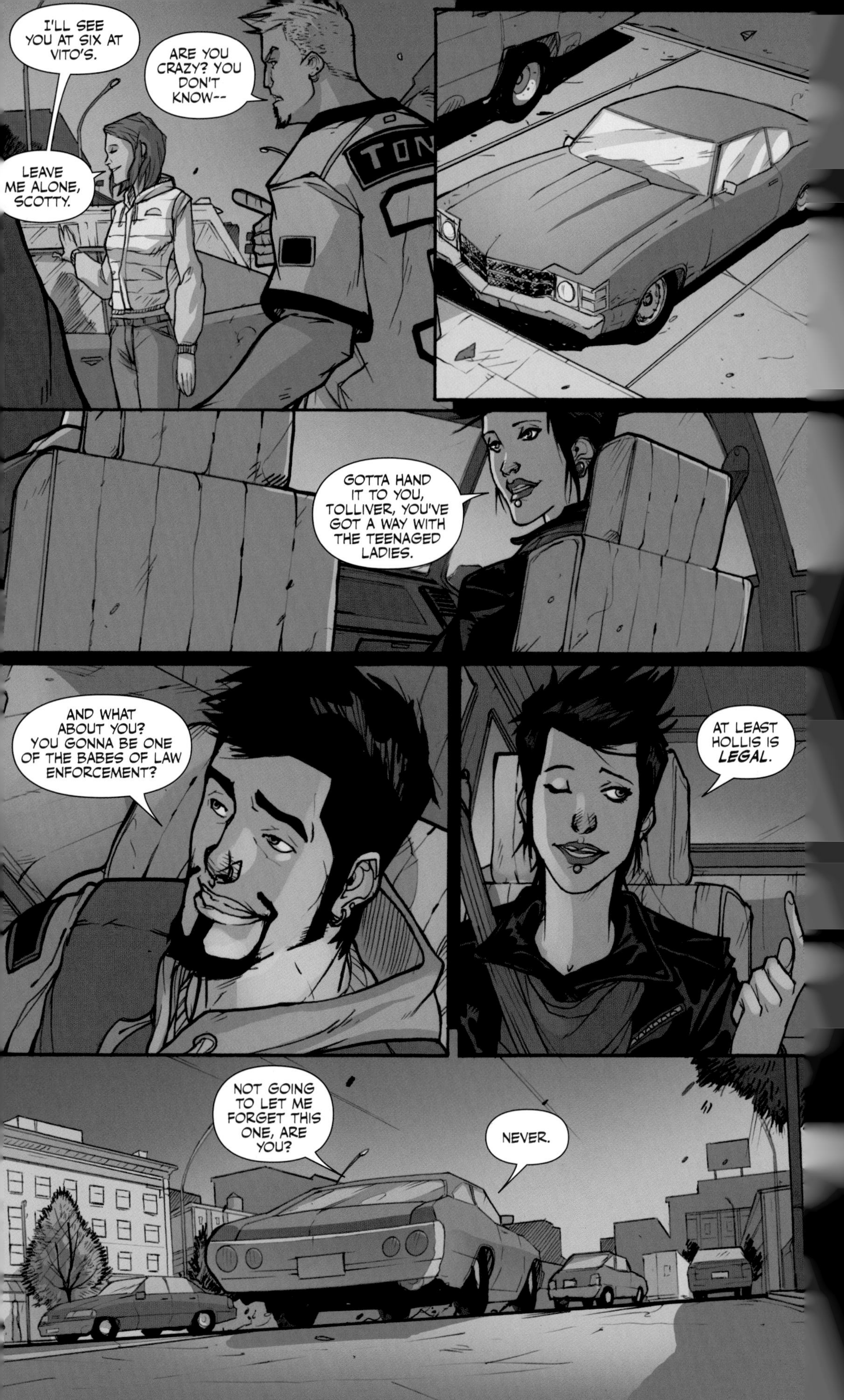
I'LL SEE YOU AT SIX AT VITO'S.
ARE YOU CRAZY? YOU DON'T KNOW--
LEAVE ME ALONE, SCOTTY.
TON
GOTTA HAND IT TO YOU, TOLLIVER, YOU'VE GOT A WAY WITH THE TEENAGED LADIES.
AND WHAT ABOUT YOU? YOU GONNA BE ONE OF THE BABES OF LAW ENFORCEMENT?
AT LEAST HOLLIS IS *LEGAL*.
NOT GOING TO LET ME FORGET THIS ONE, ARE YOU?
NEVER.

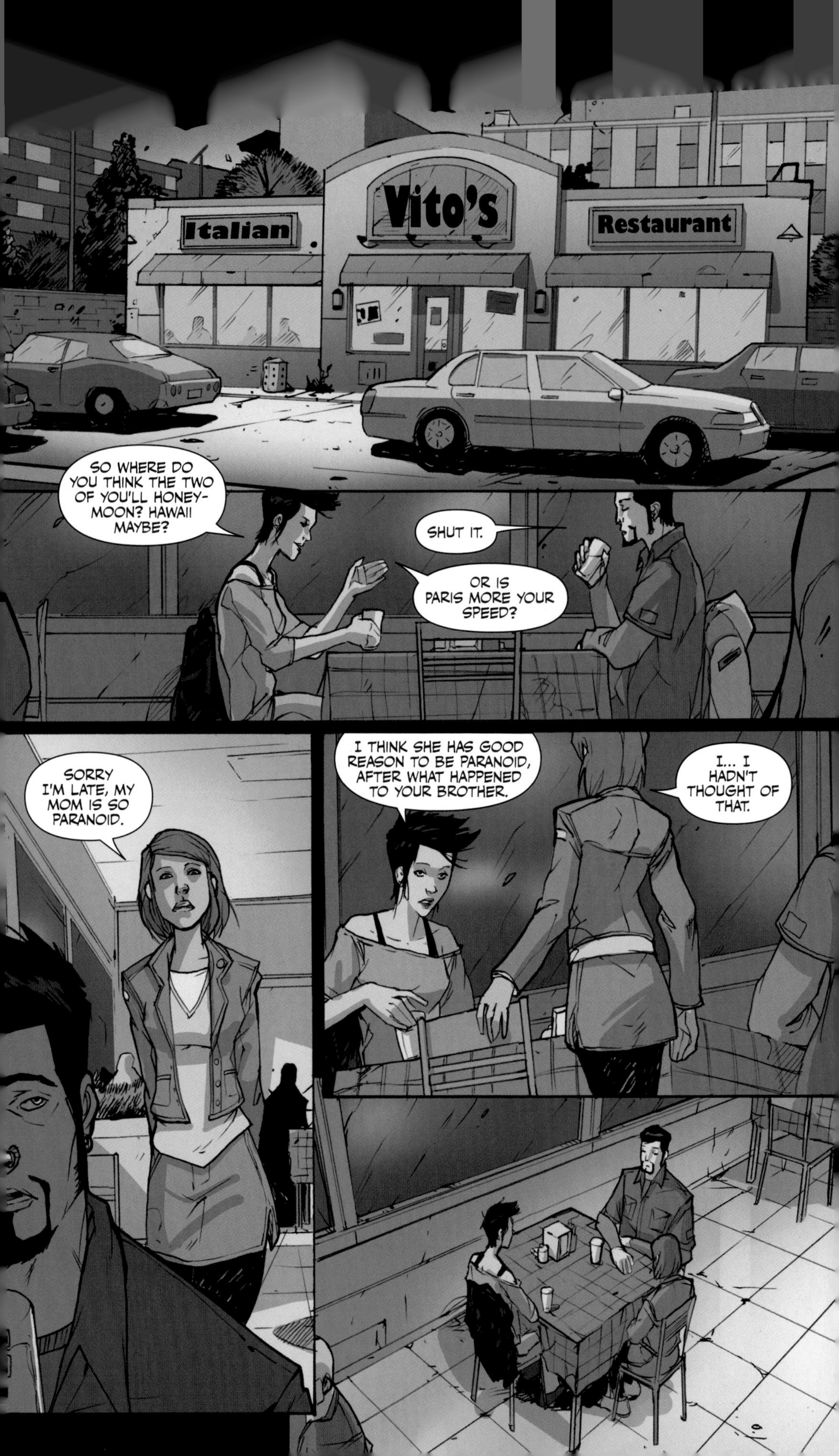
Italian
Vito's
Restaurant
SO WHERE DO YOU THINK THE TWO OF YOU'LL HONEY-MOON? HAWAII MAYBE?
SHUT IT.
OR IS PARIS MORE YOUR SPEED?
SORRY I'M LATE, MY MOM IS SO PARANOID.
I THINK SHE HAS GOOD REASON TO BE PARANOID, AFTER WHAT HAPPENED TO YOUR BROTHER.
I... I HADN'T THOUGHT OF THAT.

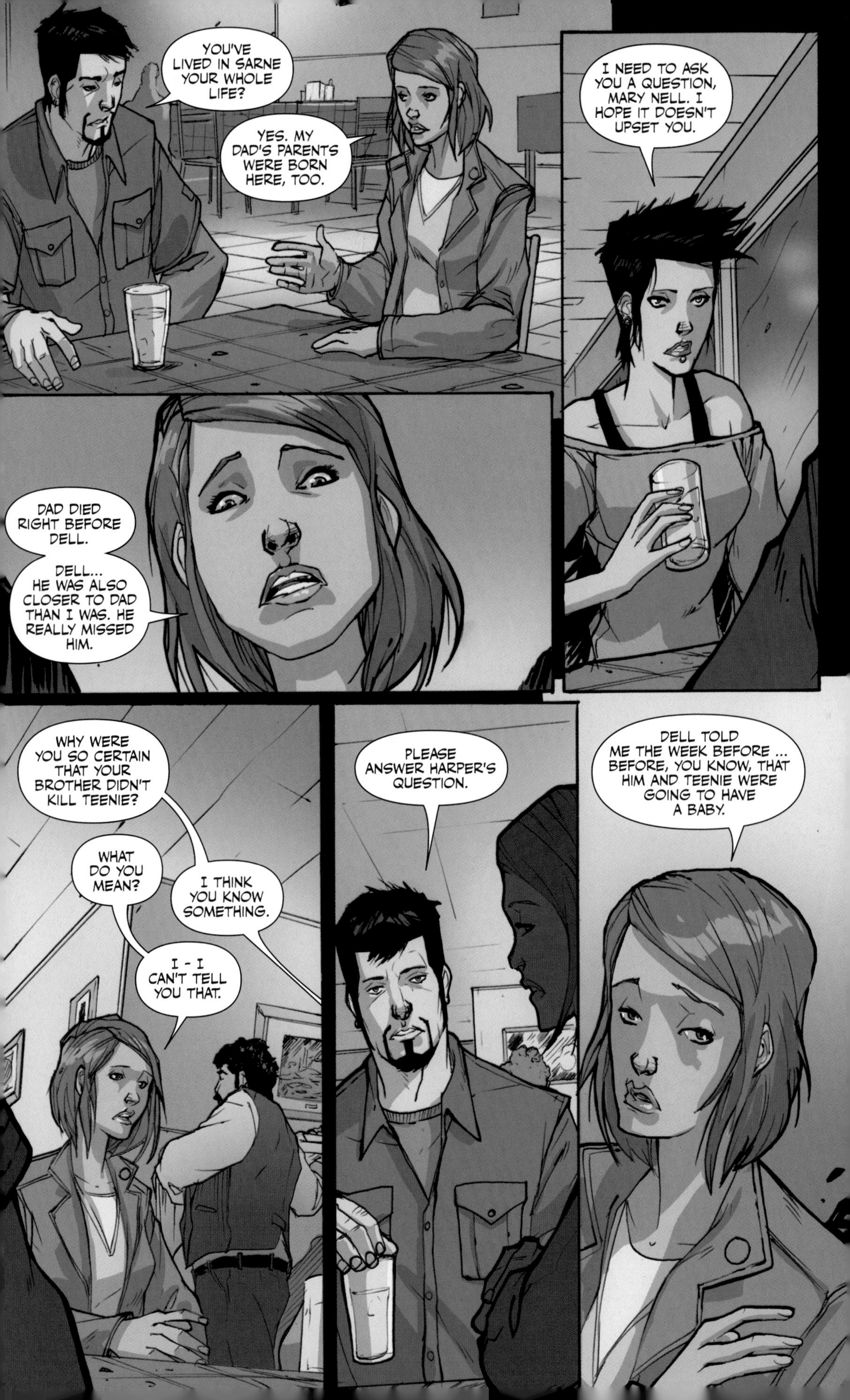
YOU'VE LIVED IN SARNE YOUR WHOLE LIFE?
YES. MY DAD'S PARENTS WERE BORN HERE, TOO.
I NEED TO ASK YOU A QUESTION, MARY NELL. I HOPE IT DOESN'T UPSET YOU.
DAD DIED RIGHT BEFORE DELL.
DELL... HE WAS ALSO CLOSER TO DAD THAN I WAS. HE REALLY MISSED HIM.
WHY WERE YOU SO CERTAIN THAT YOUR BROTHER DIDN'T KILL TEENIE?
WHAT DO YOU MEAN?
I THINK YOU KNOW SOMETHING.
I - I CAN'T TELL YOU THAT.
PLEASE ANSWER HARPER'S QUESTION.
DELL TOLD ME THE WEEK BEFORE ... BEFORE, YOU KNOW, THAT HIM AND TEENIE WERE GOING TO HAVE A BABY.

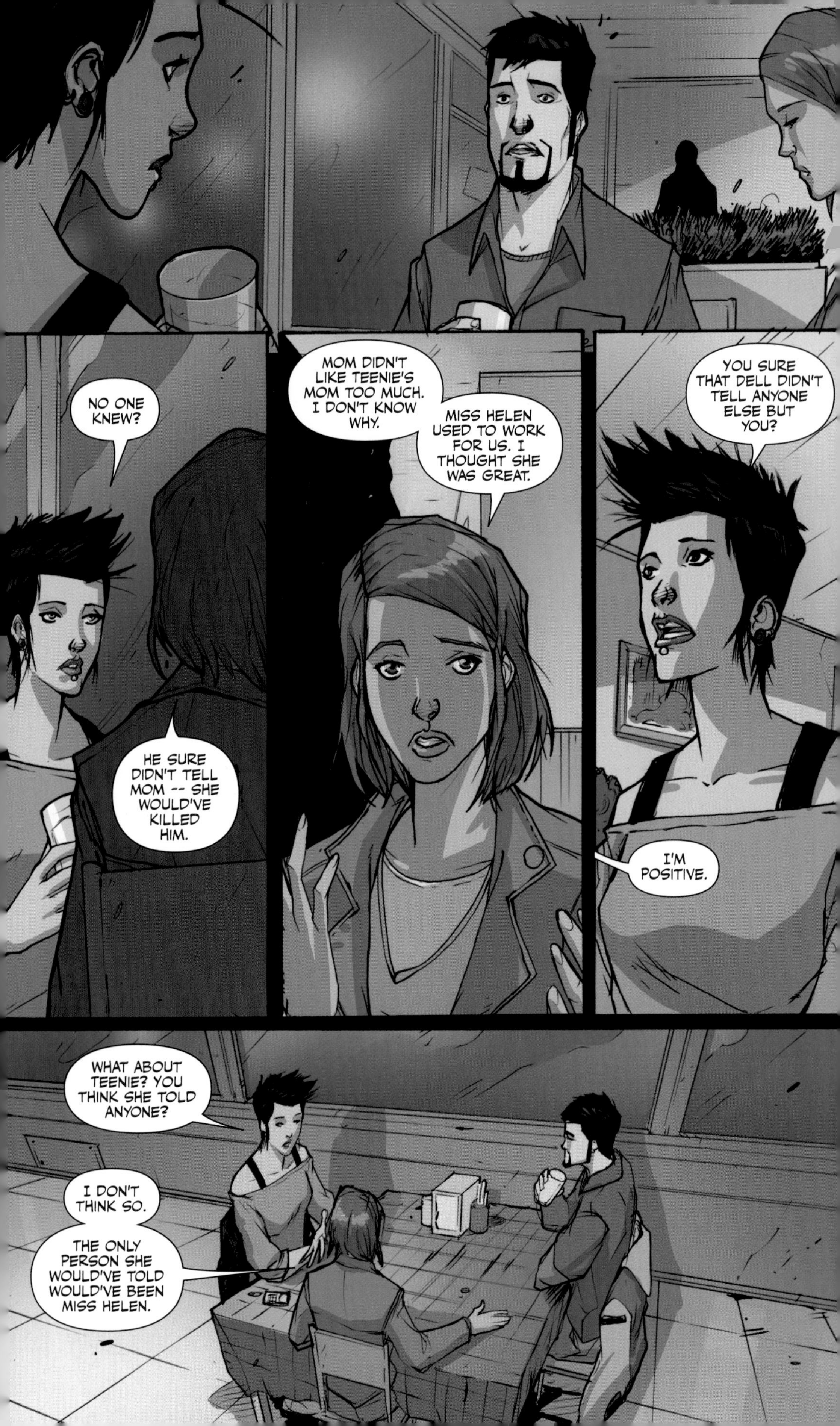
NO ONE KNEW?
HE SURE DIDN'T TELL MOM -- SHE WOULD'VE KILLED HIM.
MOM DIDN'T LIKE TEENIE'S MOM TOO MUCH. I DON'T KNOW WHY.
MISS HELEN USED TO WORK FOR US. I THOUGHT SHE WAS GREAT.
YOU SURE THAT DELL DIDN'T TELL ANYONE ELSE BUT YOU?
I'M POSITIVE.
WHAT ABOUT TEENIE? YOU THINK SHE TOLD ANYONE?
I DON'T THINK SO.
THE ONLY PERSON SHE WOULD'VE TOLD WOULD'VE BEEN MISS HELEN.

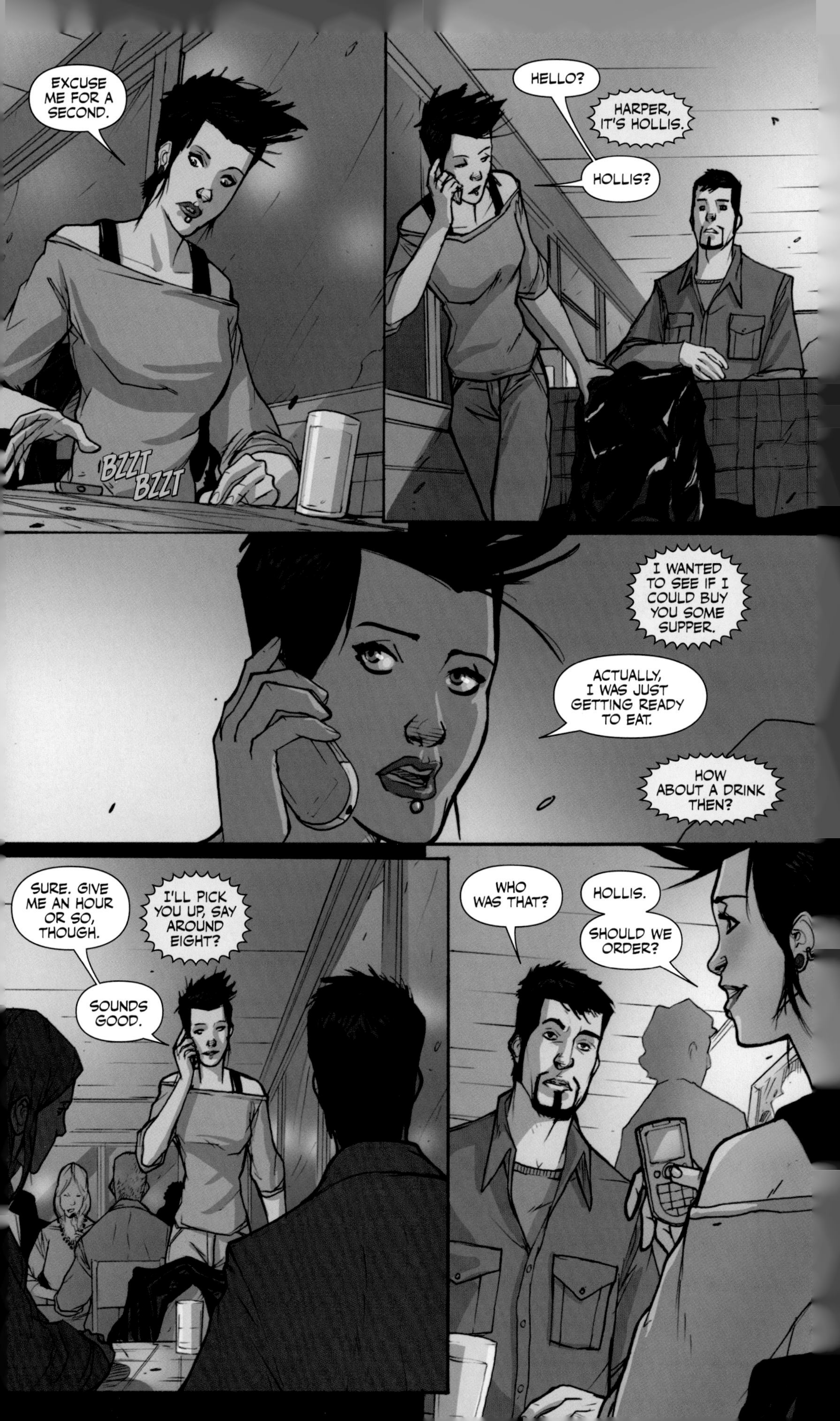
EXCUSE ME FOR A SECOND.
BZZT BZZT
HELLO?
HARPER, IT'S HOLLIS.
HOLLIS?
I WANTED TO SEE IF I COULD BUY YOU SOME SUPPER.
ACTUALLY, I WAS JUST GETTING READY TO EAT.
HOW ABOUT A DRINK THEN?
SURE. GIVE ME AN HOUR OR SO, THOUGH.
I'LL PICK YOU UP, SAY AROUND EIGHT?
SOUNDS GOOD.
WHO WAS THAT?
HOLLIS.
SHOULD WE ORDER?

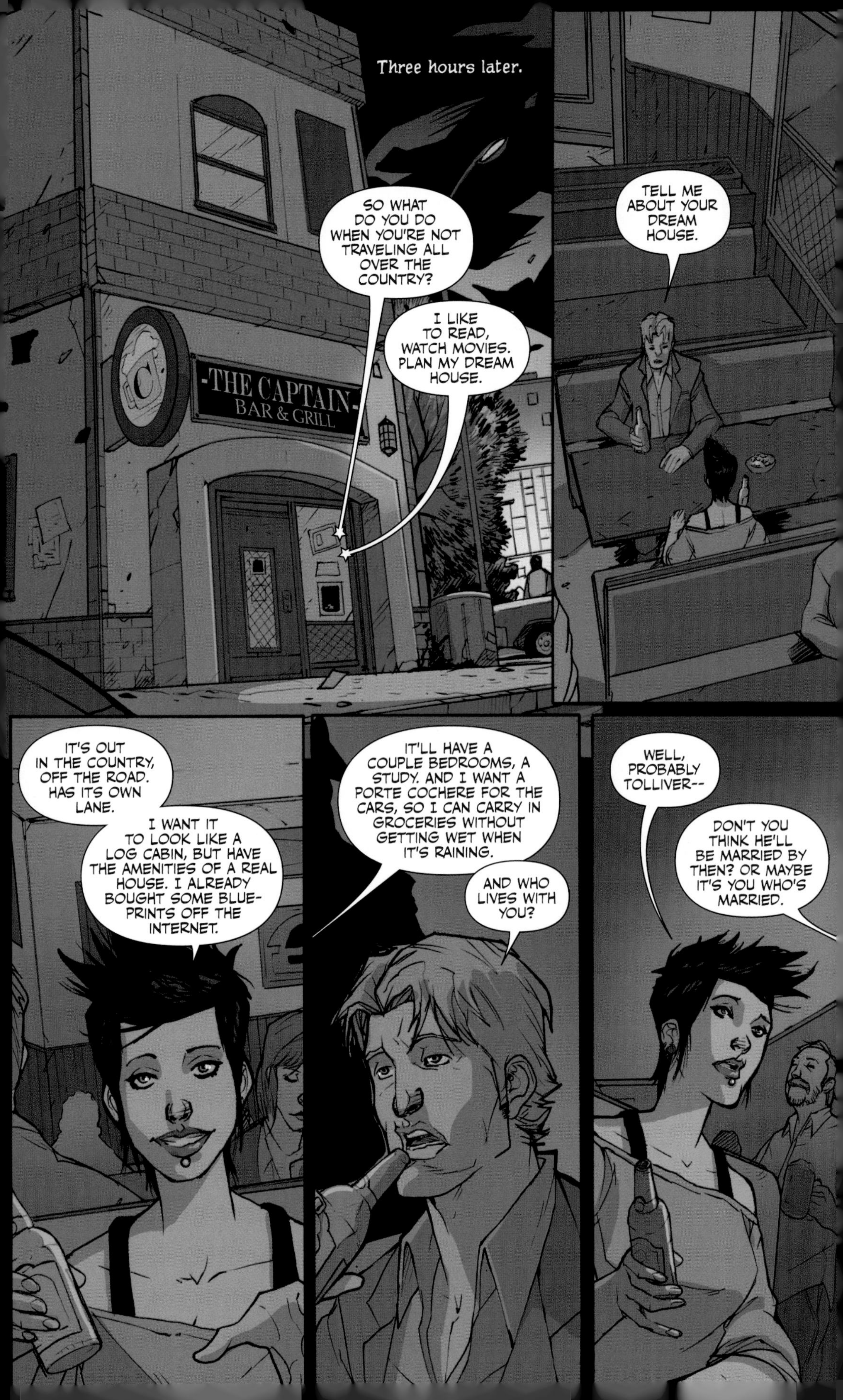

Three hours later.
SO WHAT DO YOU DO WHEN YOU'RE NOT TRAVELING ALL OVER THE COUNTRY?
I LIKE TO READ, WATCH MOVIES. PLAN MY DREAM HOUSE.
-THE CAPTAIN- BAR & GRILL
TELL ME ABOUT YOUR DREAM HOUSE.
IT'S OUT IN THE COUNTRY, OFF THE ROAD. HAS ITS OWN LANE.
I WANT IT TO LOOK LIKE A LOG CABIN, BUT HAVE THE AMENITIES OF A REAL HOUSE. I ALREADY BOUGHT SOME BLUE-PRINTS OFF THE INTERNET.
IT'LL HAVE A COUPLE BEDROOMS, A STUDY. AND I WANT A PORTE COCHERE FOR THE CARS, SO I CAN CARRY IN GROCERIES WITHOUT GETTING WET WHEN IT'S RAINING.
AND WHO LIVES WITH YOU?
WELL, PROBABLY TOLLIVER--
DON'T YOU THINK HE'LL BE MARRIED BY THEN? OR MAYBE IT'S YOU WHO'S MARRIED.

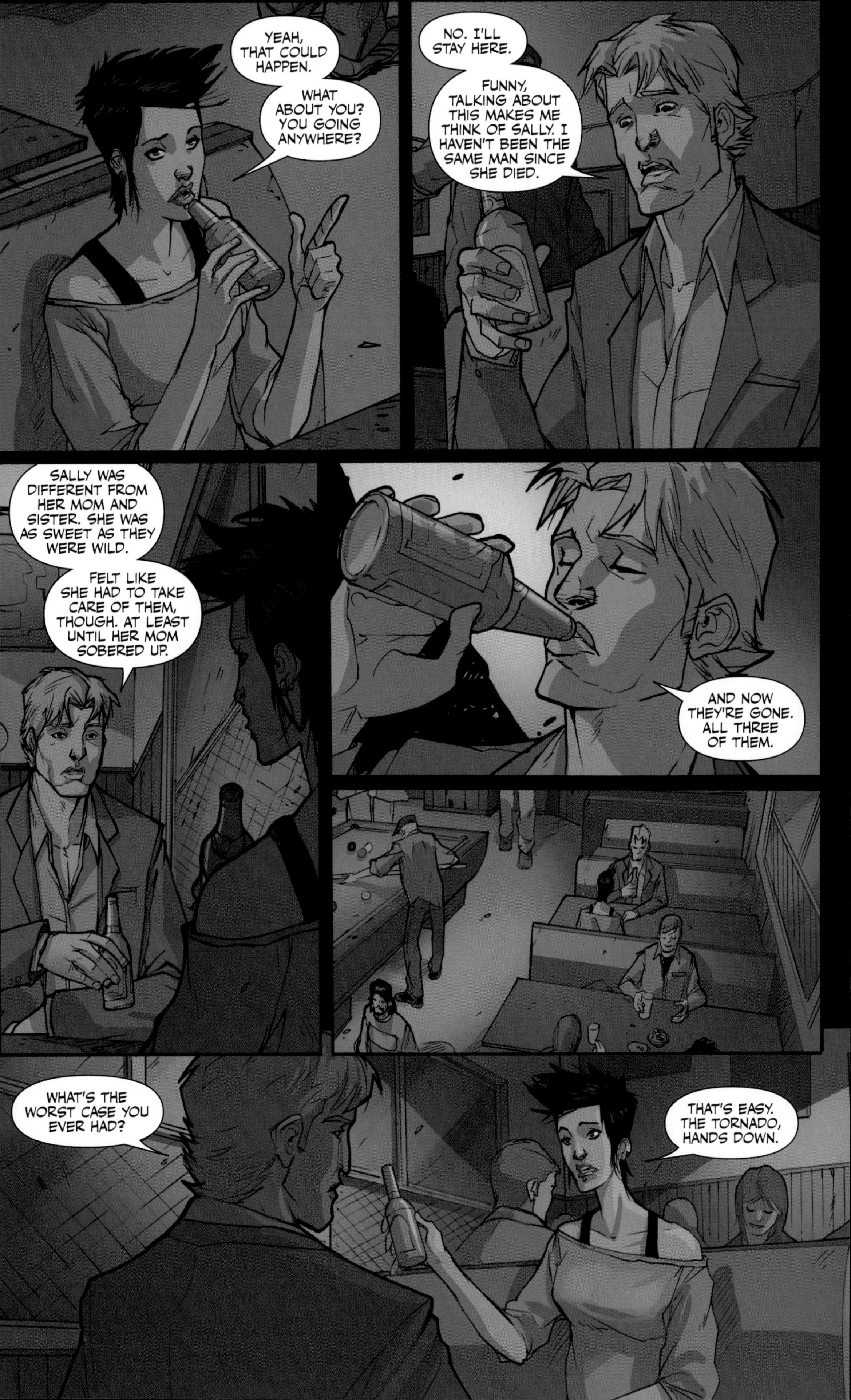
YEAH, THAT COULD HAPPEN.
WHAT ABOUT YOU? YOU GOING ANYWHERE?
NO. I'LL STAY HERE.
FUNNY, TALKING ABOUT THIS MAKES ME THINK OF SALLY. I HAVEN'T BEEN THE SAME MAN SINCE SHE DIED.
SALLY WAS DIFFERENT FROM HER MOM AND SISTER. SHE WAS AS SWEET AS THEY WERE WILD.
FELT LIKE SHE HAD TO TAKE CARE OF THEM, THOUGH. AT LEAST UNTIL HER MOM SOBERED UP.
AND NOW THEY'RE GONE. ALL THREE OF THEM.
WHAT'S THE WORST CASE YOU EVER HAD?
THAT'S EASY. THE TORNADO, HANDS DOWN.

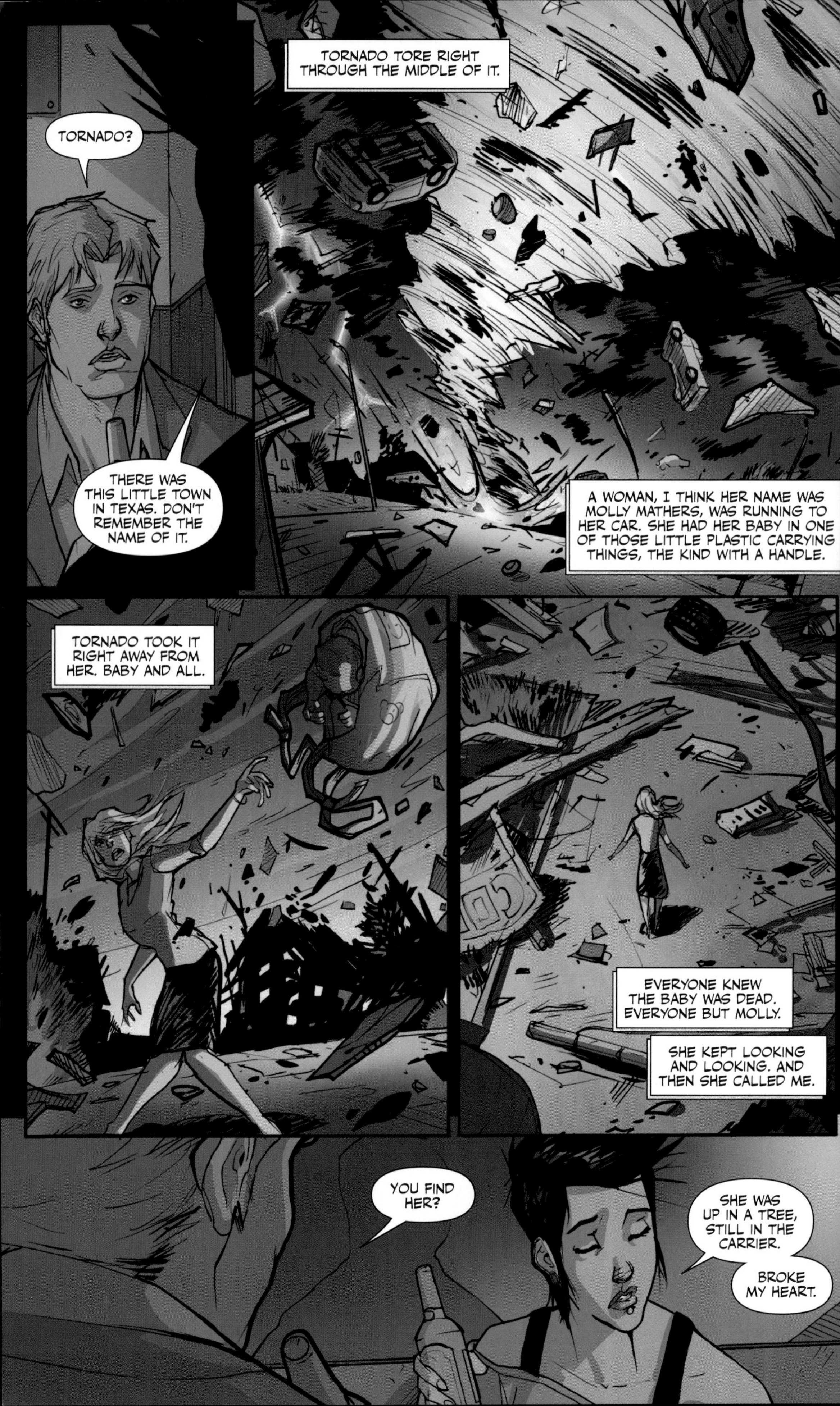
TORNADO?
TORNADO TORE RIGHT THROUGH THE MIDDLE OF IT.
THERE WAS THIS LITTLE TOWN IN TEXAS. DON'T REMEMBER THE NAME OF IT.
A WOMAN, I THINK HER NAME WAS MOLLY MATHERS, WAS RUNNING TO HER CAR. SHE HAD HER BABY IN ONE OF THOSE LITTLE PLASTIC CARRYING THINGS, THE KIND WITH A HANDLE.
TORNADO TOOK IT RIGHT AWAY FROM HER. BABY AND ALL.
EVERYONE KNEW THE BABY WAS DEAD. EVERYONE BUT MOLLY.
SHE KEPT LOOKING AND LOOKING. AND THEN SHE CALLED ME.
YOU FIND HER?
SHE WAS UP IN A TREE, STILL IN THE CARRIER.
BROKE MY HEART.

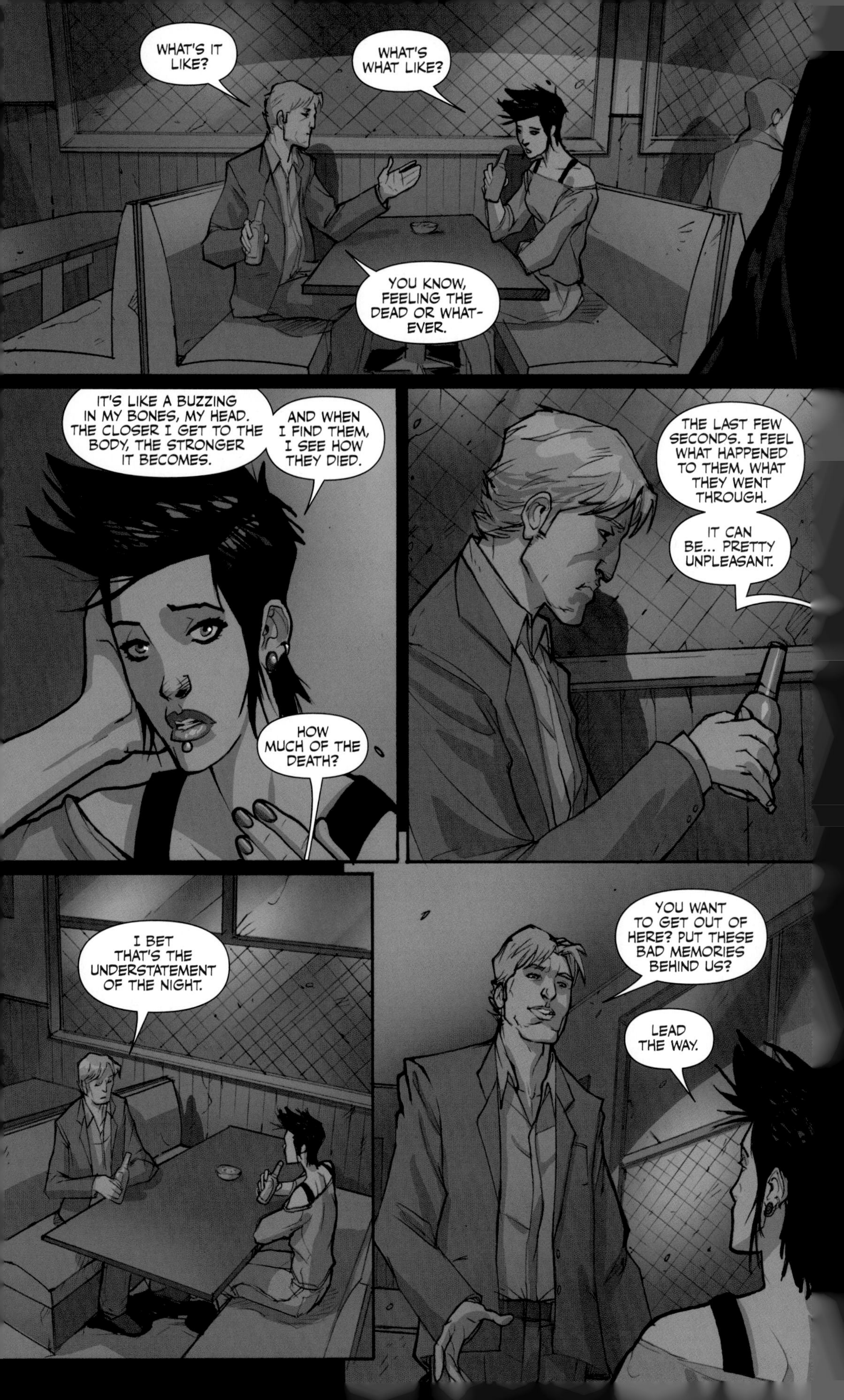
WHAT'S IT LIKE?
WHAT'S WHAT LIKE?
YOU KNOW, FEELING THE DEAD OR WHAT-EVER.
IT'S LIKE A BUZZING IN MY BONES, MY HEAD. THE CLOSER I GET TO THE BODY, THE STRONGER IT BECOMES.
AND WHEN I FIND THEM, I SEE HOW THEY DIED.
HOW MUCH OF THE DEATH?
THE LAST FEW SECONDS. I FEEL WHAT HAPPENED TO THEM, WHAT THEY WENT THROUGH.
IT CAN BE... PRETTY UNPLEASANT.
I BET THAT'S THE UNDERSTATEMENT OF THE NIGHT.
YOU WANT TO GET OUT OF HERE? PUT THESE BAD MEMORIES BEHIND US?
LEAD THE WAY.

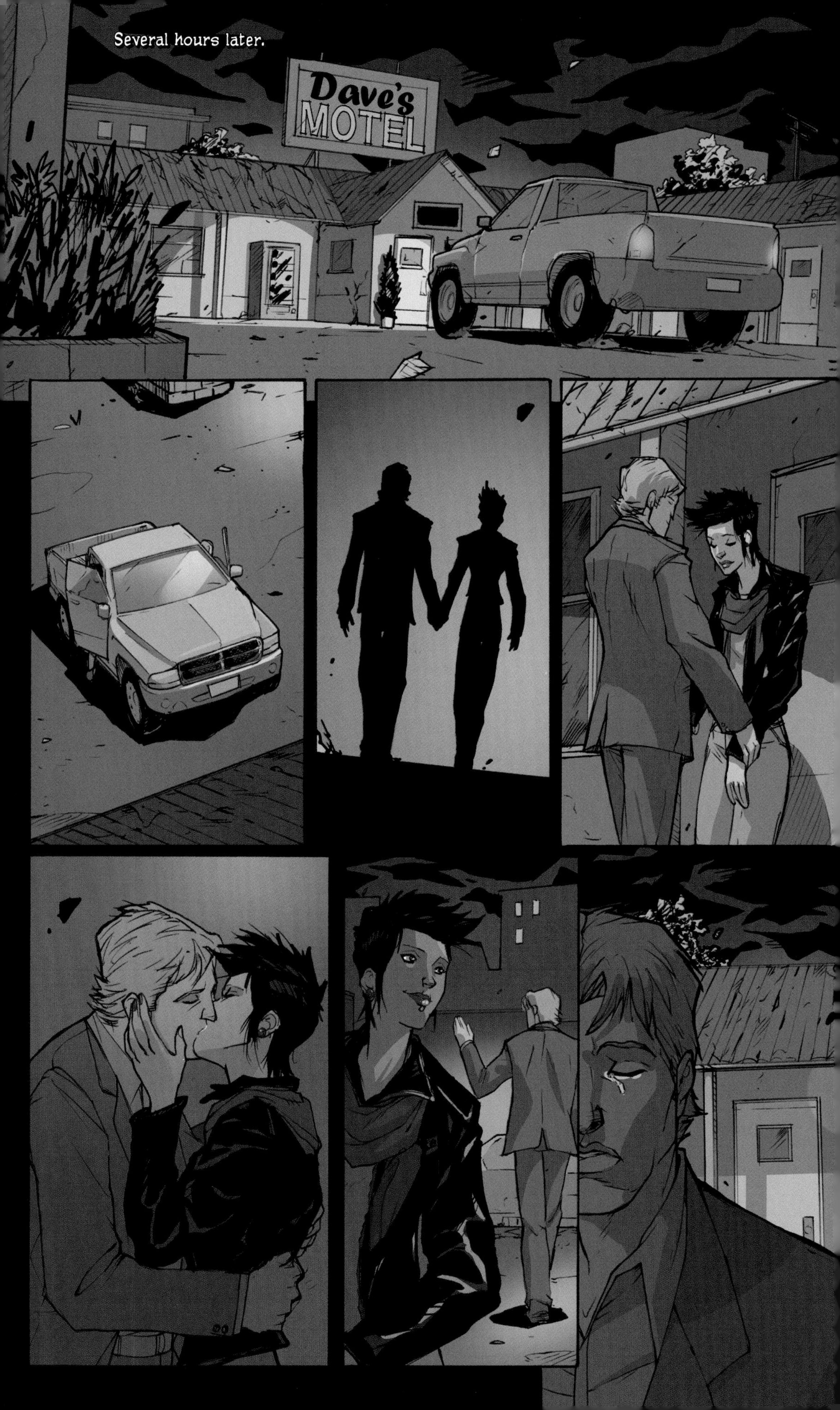
Several hours later.
Dave's
MOTEL

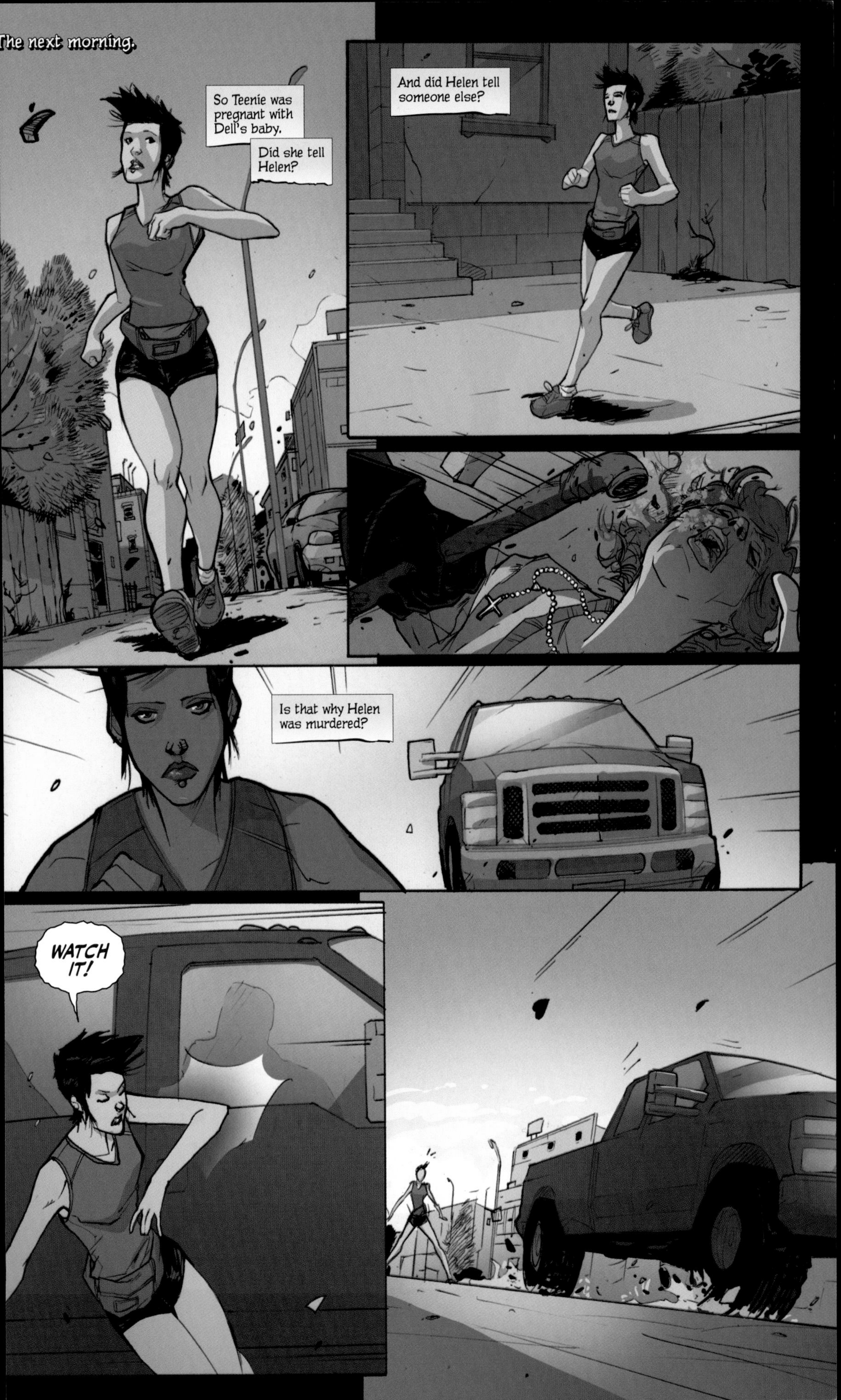
The next morning.
So Teenie was pregnant with Dell's baby.
Did she tell Helen?
And did Helen tell someone else?
Is that why Helen was murdered?
WATCH IT!

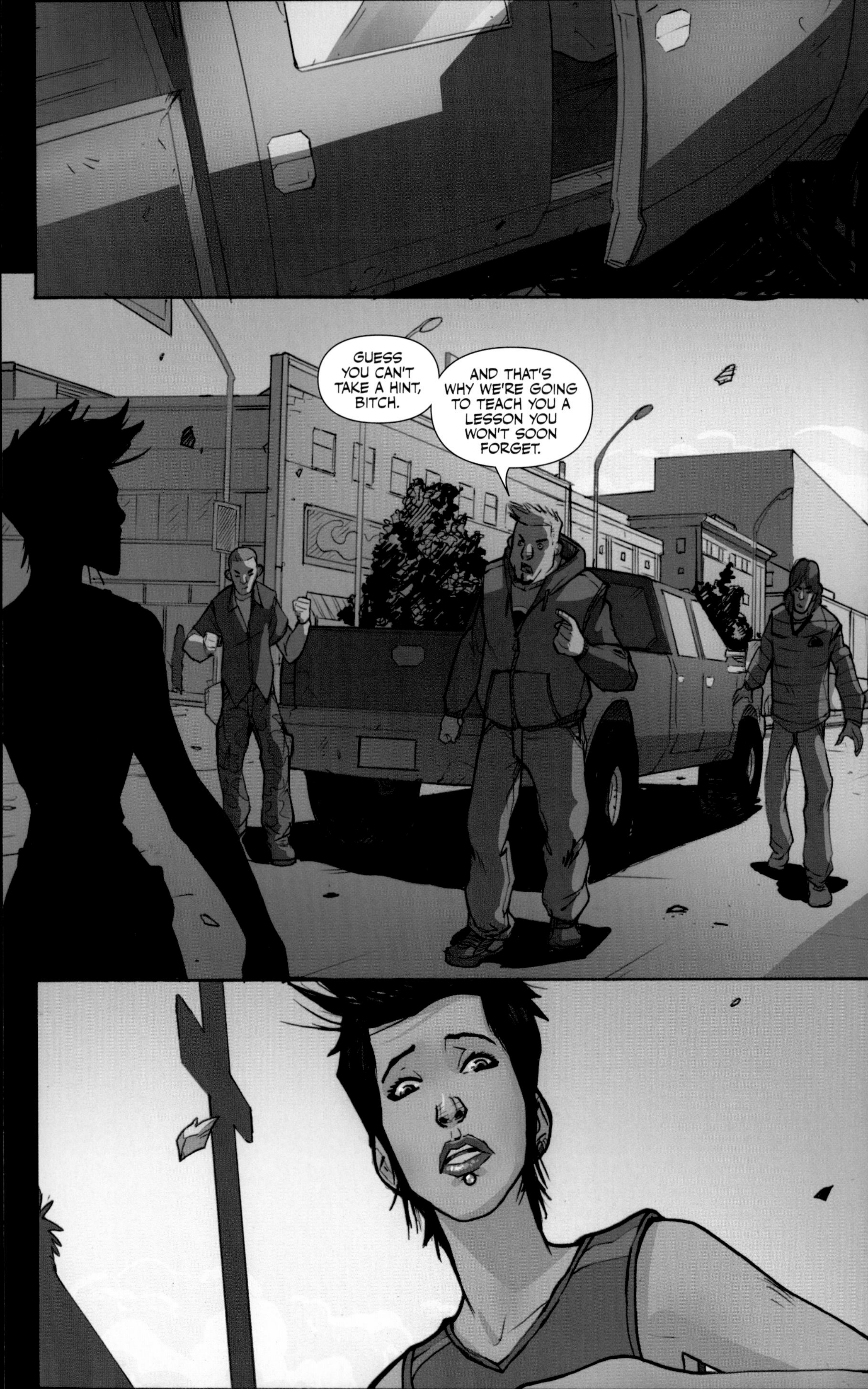
GUESS YOU CAN'T TAKE A HINT, BITCH.
AND THAT'S WHY WE'RE GOING TO TEACH YOU A LESSON YOU WON'T SOON FORGET.

CHAPTER FOUR

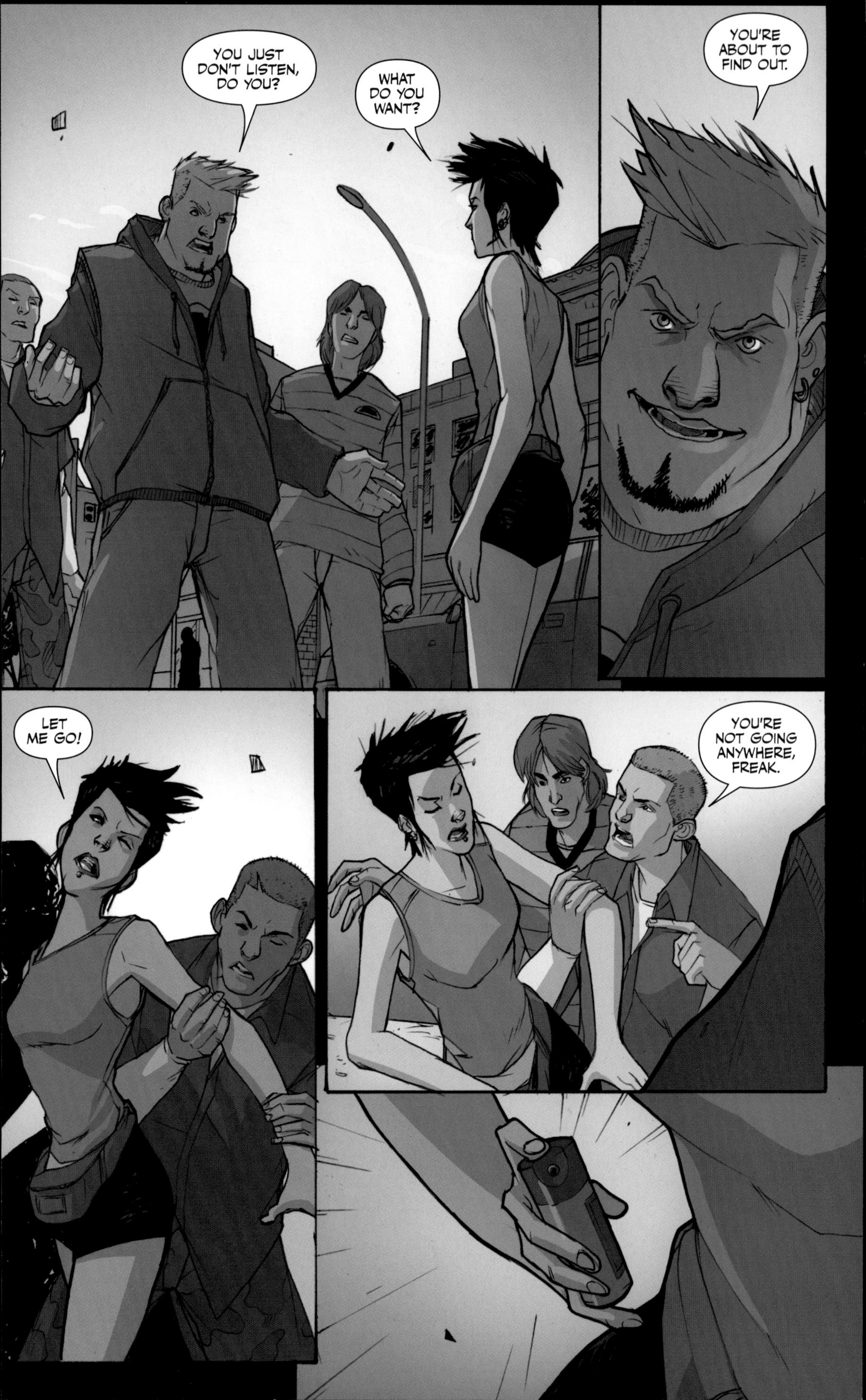
YOU JUST DON'T LISTEN, DO YOU?
WHAT DO YOU WANT?
YOU'RE ABOUT TO FIND OUT.
LET ME GO!
YOU'RE NOT GOING ANYWHERE, FREAK.

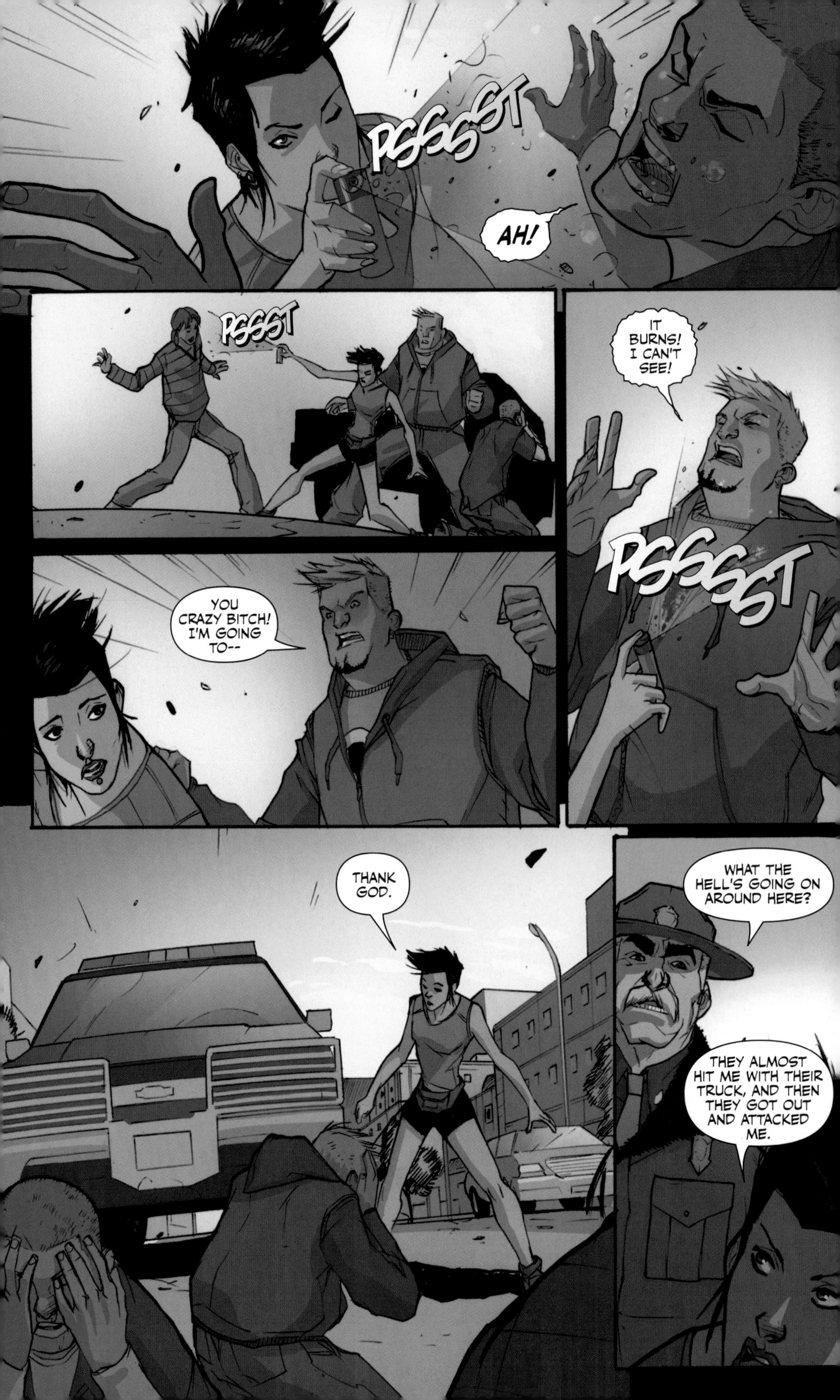
PSSSST
AH!
PSSST
IT BURNS! I CAN'T SEE!
YOU CRAZY BITCH! I'M GOING TO--
PSSSST
THANK GOD.
WHAT THE HELL'S GOING ON AROUND HERE?
THEY ALMOST HIT ME WITH THEIR TRUCK, AND THEN THEY GOT OUT AND ATTACKED ME.

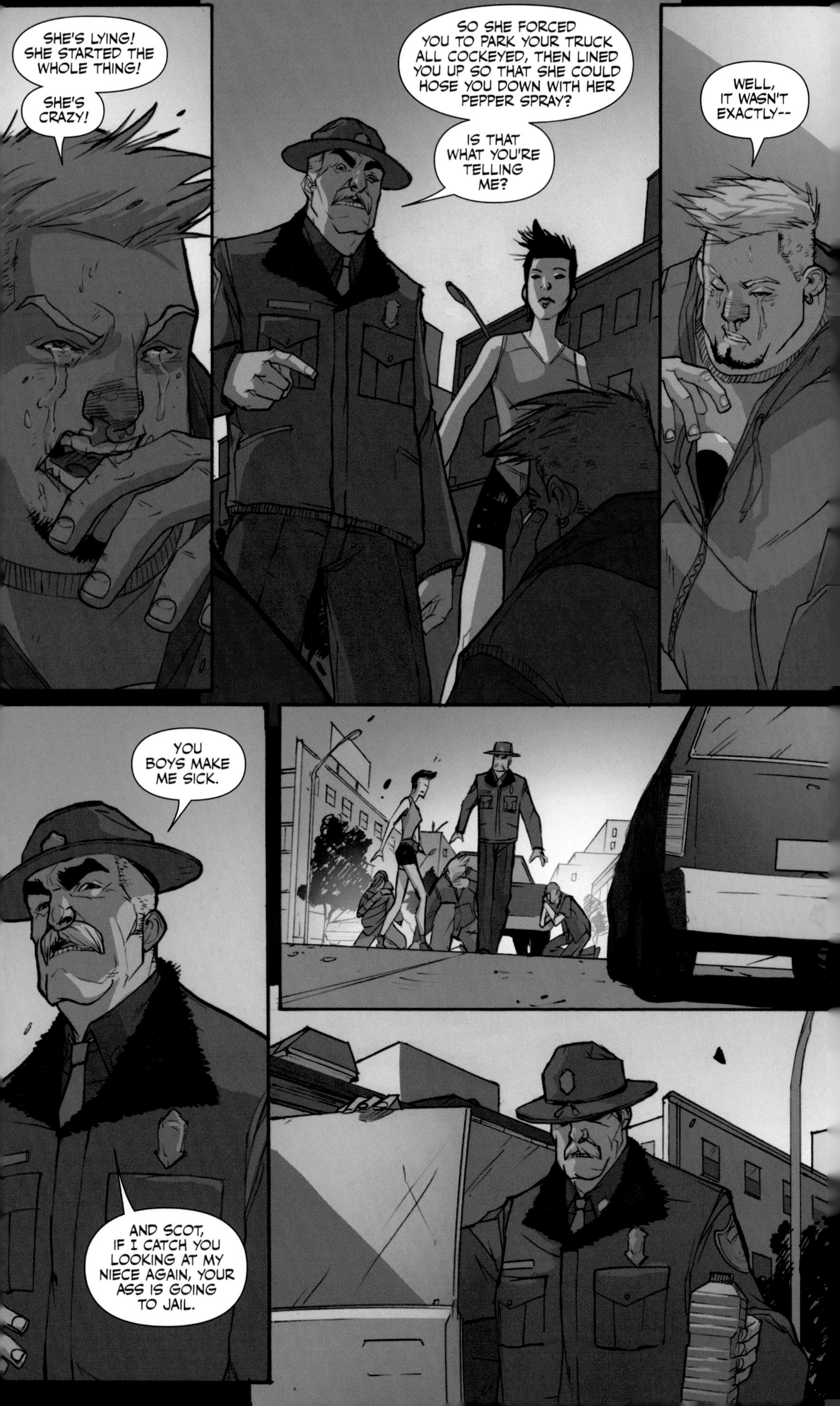
SHE'S LYING! SHE STARTED THE WHOLE THING!
SHE'S CRAZY!
SO SHE FORCED YOU TO PARK YOUR TRUCK ALL COCKEYED, THEN LINED YOU UP SO THAT SHE COULD HOSE YOU DOWN WITH HER PEPPER SPRAY?
IS THAT WHAT YOU'RE TELLING ME?
WELL, IT WASN'T EXACTLY--
YOU BOYS MAKE ME SICK.
AND SCOT, IF I CATCH YOU LOOKING AT MY NIECE AGAIN, YOUR ASS IS GOING TO JAIL.

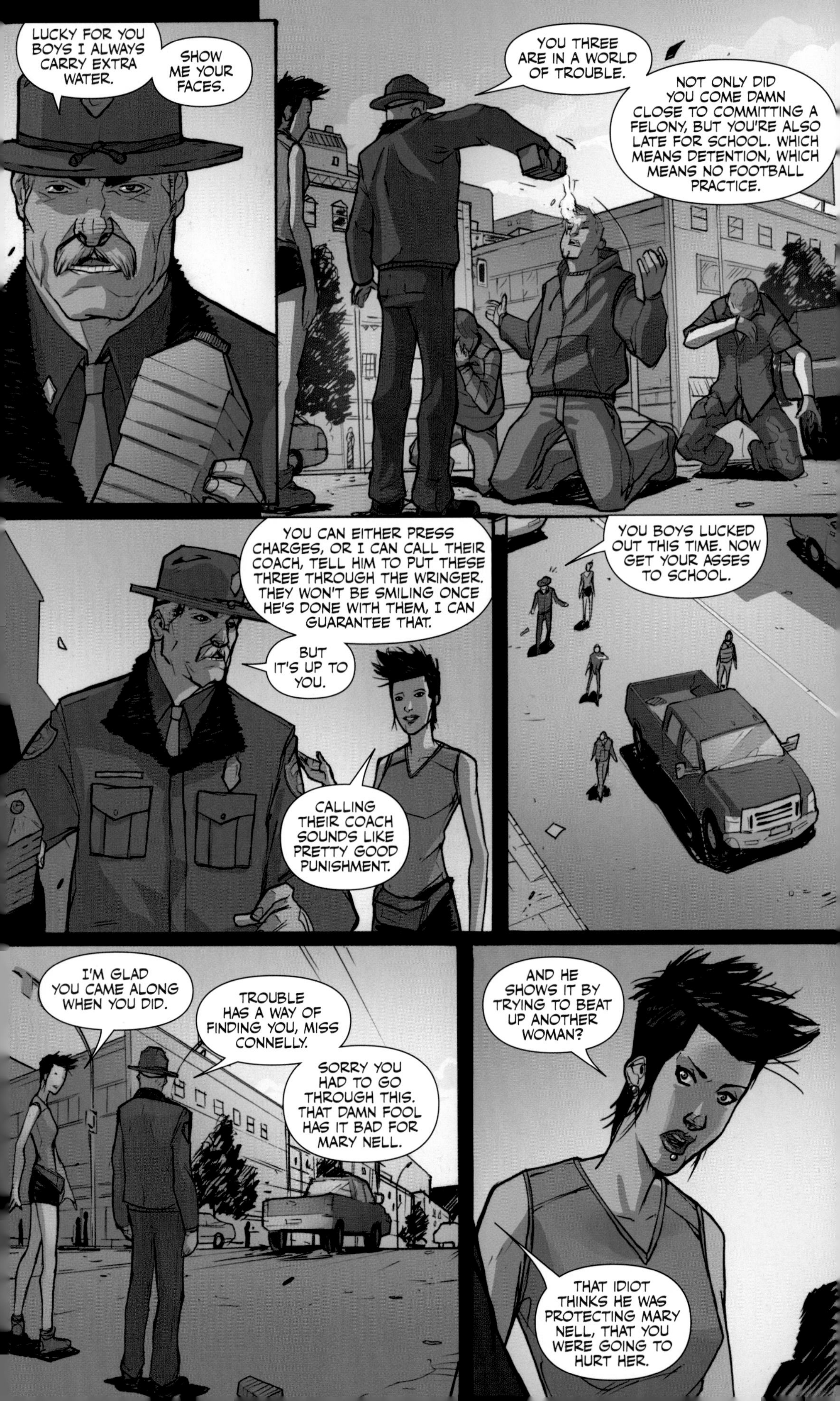
LUCKY FOR YOU BOYS I ALWAYS CARRY EXTRA WATER.
SHOW ME YOUR FACES.
YOU THREE ARE IN A WORLD OF TROUBLE.
NOT ONLY DID YOU COME DAMN CLOSE TO COMMITTING A FELONY, BUT YOU'RE ALSO LATE FOR SCHOOL. WHICH MEANS DETENTION, WHICH MEANS NO FOOTBALL PRACTICE.
YOU CAN EITHER PRESS CHARGES, OR I CAN CALL THEIR COACH, TELL HIM TO PUT THESE THREE THROUGH THE WRINGER. THEY WON'T BE SMILING ONCE HE'S DONE WITH THEM, I CAN GUARANTEE THAT.
BUT IT'S UP TO YOU.
CALLING THEIR COACH SOUNDS LIKE PRETTY GOOD PUNISHMENT.
YOU BOYS LUCKED OUT THIS TIME. NOW GET YOUR ASSES TO SCHOOL.
I'M GLAD YOU CAME ALONG WHEN YOU DID.
TROUBLE HAS A WAY OF FINDING YOU, MISS CONNELLY.
SORRY YOU HAD TO GO THROUGH THIS. THAT DAMN FOOL HAS IT BAD FOR MARY NELL.
AND HE SHOWS IT BY TRYING TO BEAT UP ANOTHER WOMAN?
THAT IDIOT THINKS HE WAS PROTECTING MARY NELL, THAT YOU WERE GOING TO HURT HER.

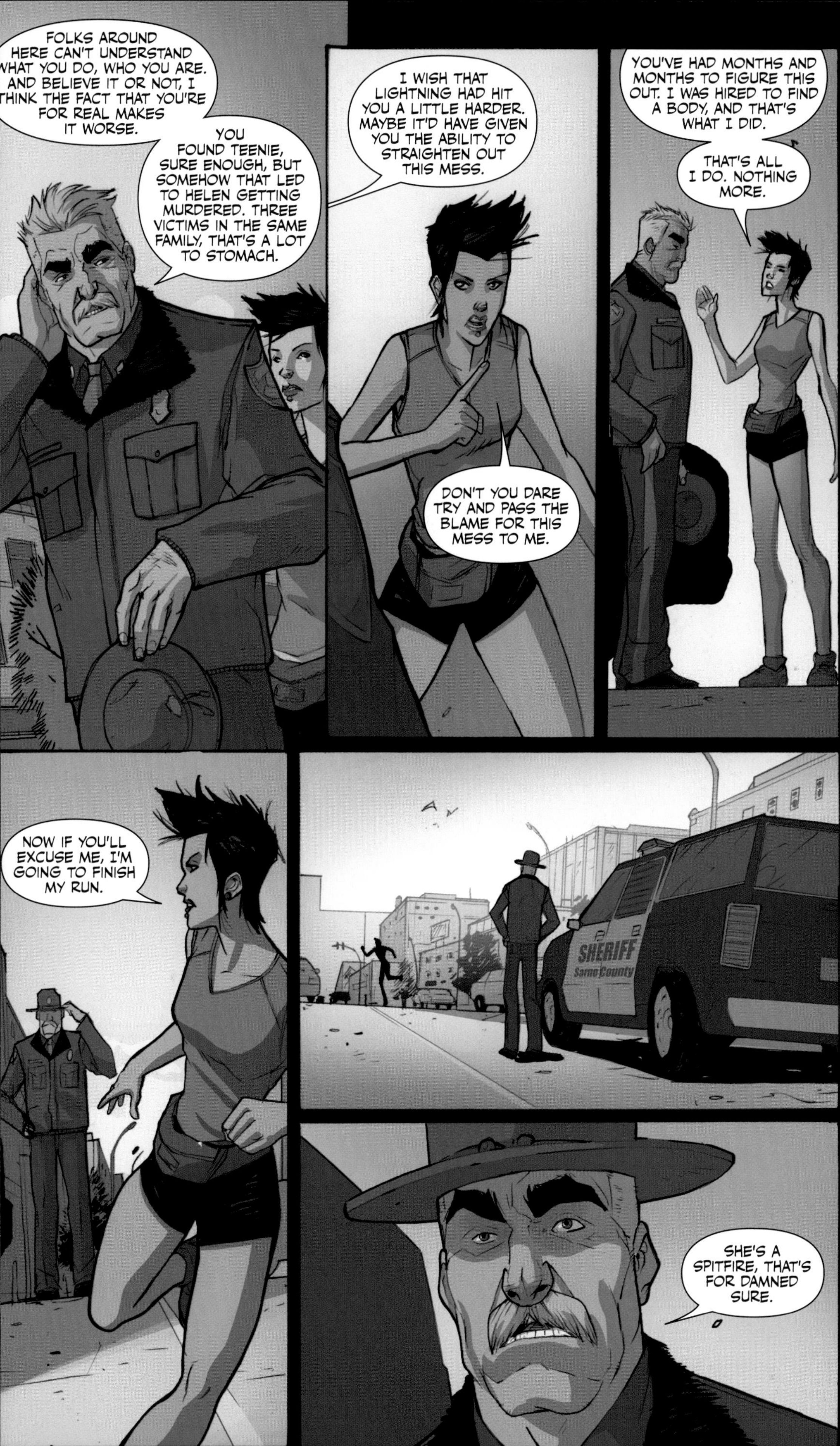
FOLKS AROUND HERE CAN'T UNDERSTAND WHAT YOU DO, WHO YOU ARE. AND BELIEVE IT OR NOT, I THINK THE FACT THAT YOU'RE FOR REAL MAKES IT WORSE.
YOU FOUND TEENIE, SURE ENOUGH, BUT SOMEHOW THAT LED TO HELEN GETTING MURDERED. THREE VICTIMS IN THE SAME FAMILY, THAT'S A LOT TO STOMACH.
I WISH THAT LIGHTNING HAD HIT YOU A LITTLE HARDER. MAYBE IT'D HAVE GIVEN YOU THE ABILITY TO STRAIGHTEN OUT THIS MESS.
DON'T YOU DARE TRY AND PASS THE BLAME FOR THIS MESS TO ME.
YOU'VE HAD MONTHS AND MONTHS TO FIGURE THIS OUT. I WAS HIRED TO FIND A BODY, AND THAT'S WHAT I DID.
THAT'S ALL I DO. NOTHING MORE.
NOW IF YOU'LL EXCUSE ME, I'M GOING TO FINISH MY RUN.
SHERIFF
Sarno County
SHE'S A SPITFIRE, THAT'S FOR DAMNED SURE.

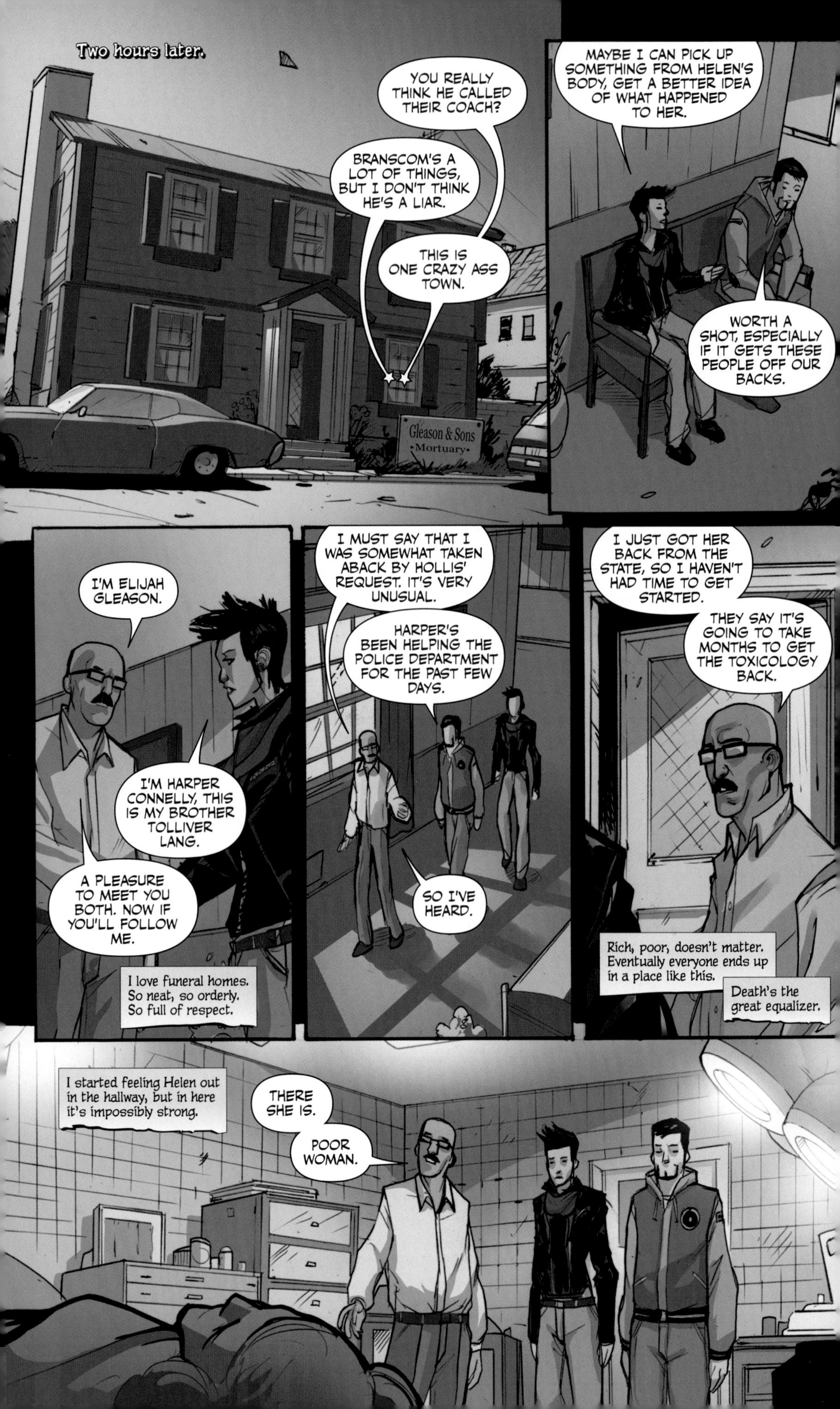
Two hours later.
YOU REALLY THINK HE CALLED THEIR COACH?
BRANSCOM'S A LOT OF THINGS, BUT I DON'T THINK HE'S A LIAR.
THIS IS ONE CRAZY ASS TOWN.
Gleason & Sons
Mortuary
MAYBE I CAN PICK UP SOMETHING FROM HELEN'S BODY, GET A BETTER IDEA OF WHAT HAPPENED TO HER.
WORTH A SHOT, ESPECIALLY IF IT GETS THESE PEOPLE OFF OUR BACKS.
I'M ELIJAH GLEASON.
I'M HARPER CONNELLY, THIS IS MY BROTHER TOLLIVER LANG.
A PLEASURE TO MEET YOU BOTH. NOW IF YOU'LL FOLLOW ME.
I love funeral homes. So neat, so orderly. So full of respect.
I MUST SAY THAT I WAS SOMEWHAT TAKEN ABACK BY HOLLIS' REQUEST. IT'S VERY UNUSUAL.
HARPER'S BEEN HELPING THE POLICE DEPARTMENT FOR THE PAST FEW DAYS.
SO I'VE HEARD.
I JUST GOT HER BACK FROM THE STATE, SO I HAVEN'T HAD TIME TO GET STARTED.
THEY SAY IT'S GOING TO TAKE MONTHS TO GET THE TOXICOLOGY BACK.
Rich, poor, doesn't matter. Eventually everyone ends up in a place like this.
Death's the great equalizer.
I started feeling Helen out in the hallway, but in here it's impossibly strong.
THERE SHE IS.
POOR WOMAN.

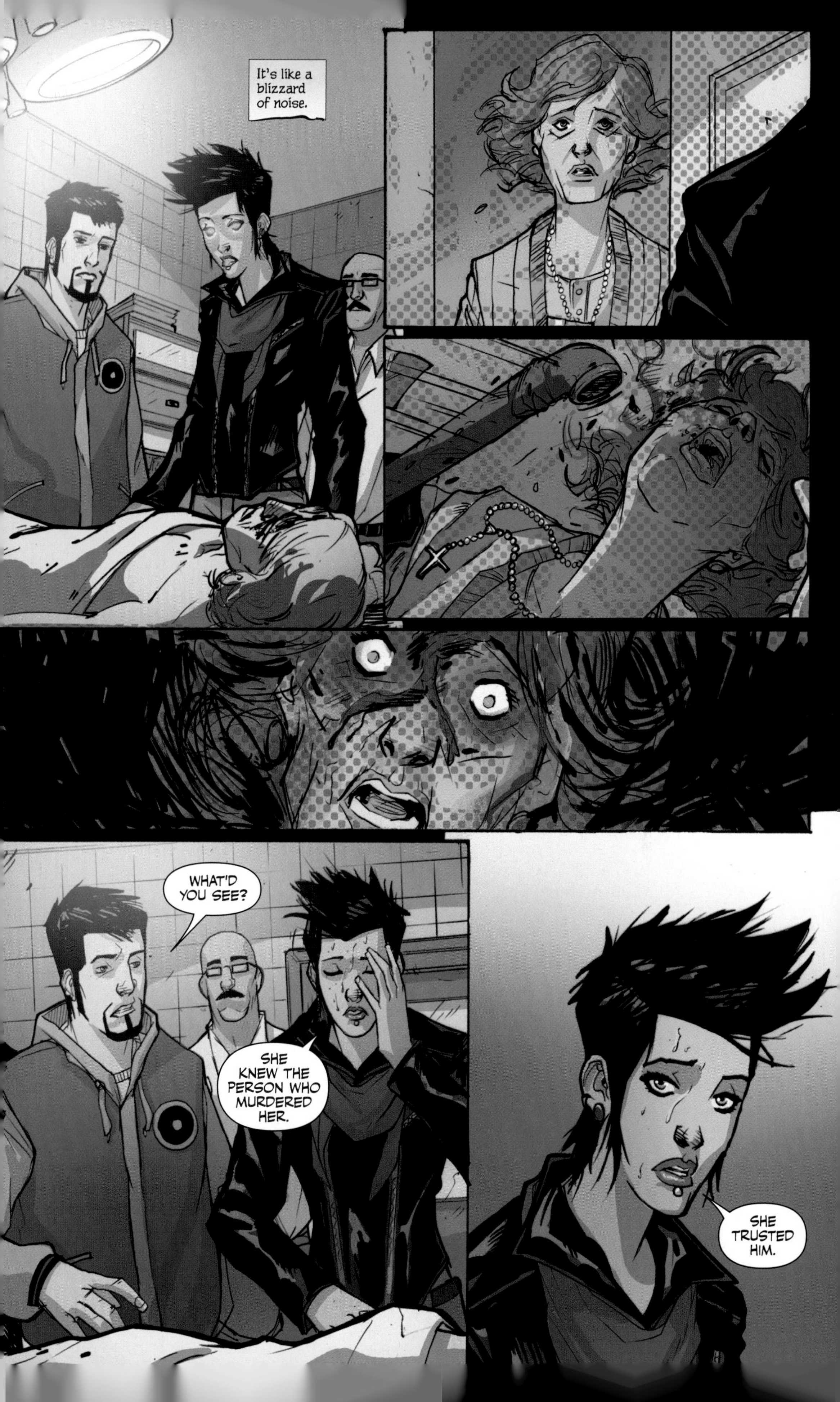
It's like a blizzard of noise.
WHAT'D YOU SEE?
SHE KNEW THE PERSON WHO MURDERED HER.
SHE TRUSTED HIM.

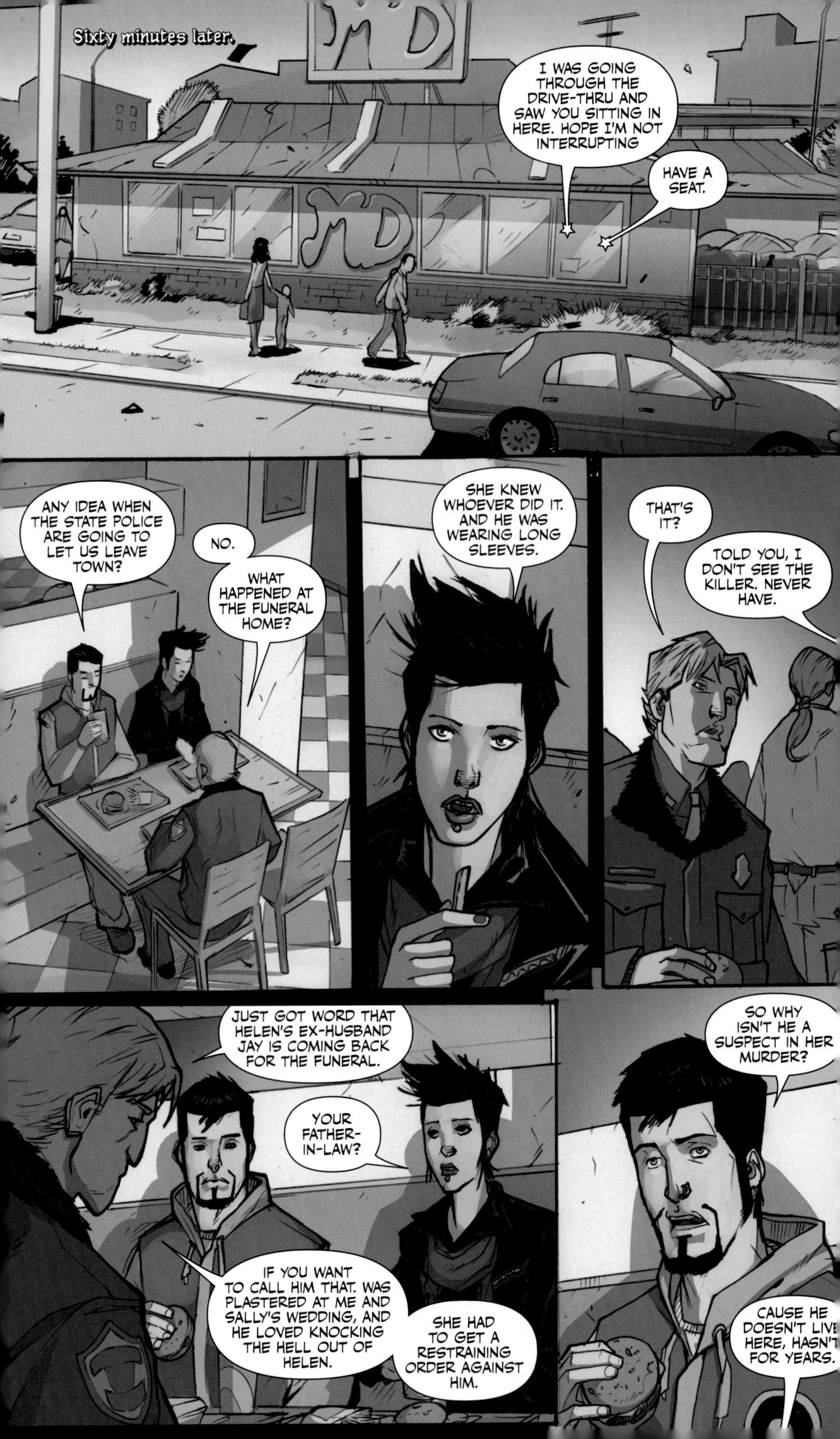
Sixty minutes later.
I WAS GOING THROUGH THE DRIVE-THRU AND SAW YOU SITTING IN HERE. HOPE I'M NOT INTERRUPTING
HAVE A SEAT.
ANY IDEA WHEN THE STATE POLICE ARE GOING TO LET US LEAVE TOWN?
NO.
WHAT HAPPENED AT THE FUNERAL HOME?
SHE KNEW WHOEVER DID IT. AND HE WAS WEARING LONG SLEEVES.
THAT'S IT?
TOLD YOU, I DON'T SEE THE KILLER. NEVER HAVE.
JUST GOT WORD THAT HELEN'S EX-HUSBAND JAY IS COMING BACK FOR THE FUNERAL.
YOUR FATHER-IN-LAW?
IF YOU WANT TO CALL HIM THAT. WAS PLASTERED AT ME AND SALLY'S WEDDING, AND HE LOVED KNOCKING THE HELL OUT OF HELEN.
SHE HAD TO GET A RESTRAINING ORDER AGAINST HIM.
SO WHY ISN'T HE A SUSPECT IN HER MURDER?
CAUSE HE DOESN'T LIVE HERE, HASN'T FOR YEARS.

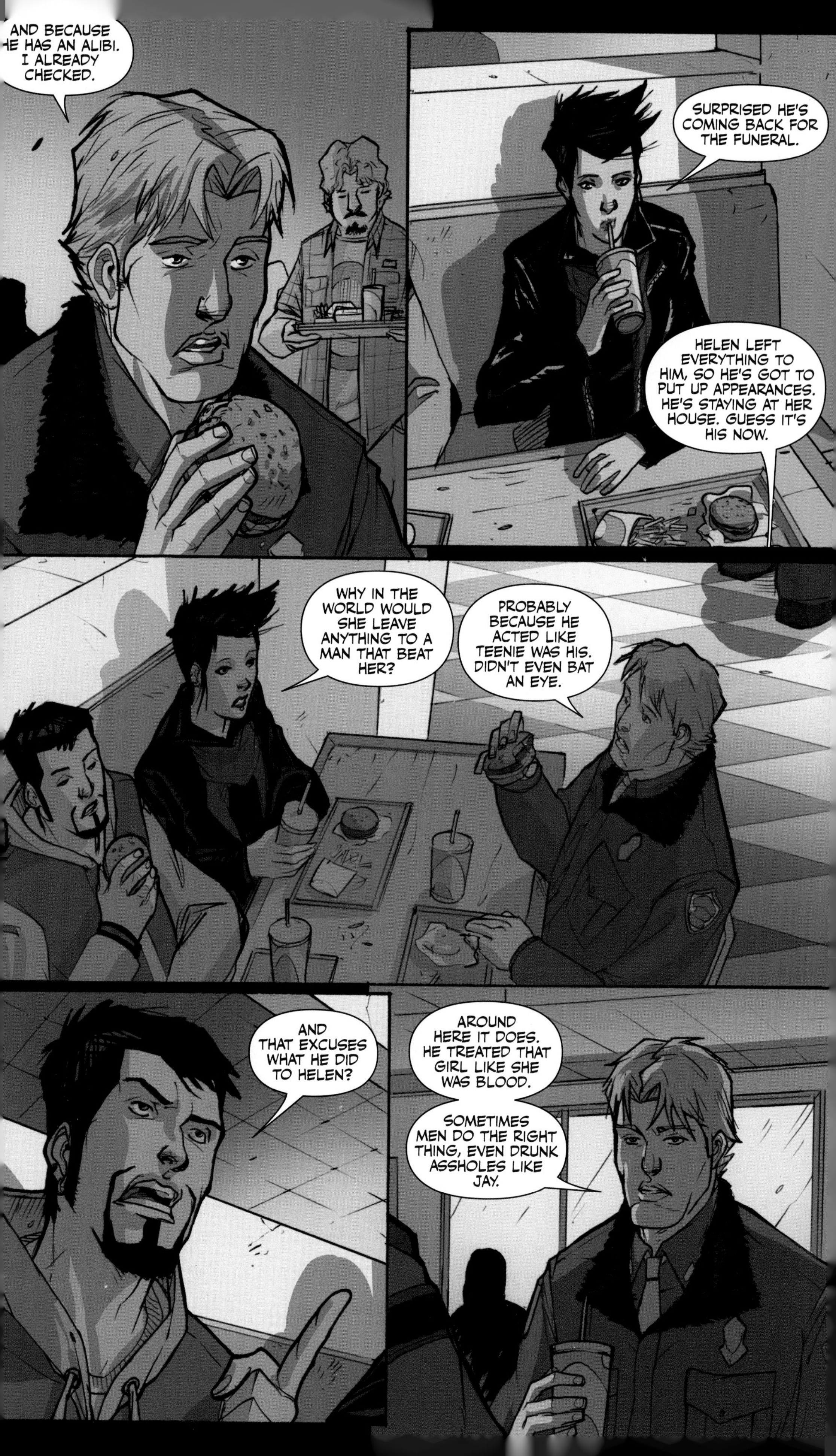
AND BECAUSE HE HAS AN ALIBI. I ALREADY CHECKED.
SURPRISED HE'S COMING BACK FOR THE FUNERAL.
HELEN LEFT EVERYTHING TO HIM, SO HE'S GOT TO PUT UP APPEARANCES. HE'S STAYING AT HER HOUSE. GUESS IT'S HIS NOW.
WHY IN THE WORLD WOULD SHE LEAVE ANYTHING TO A MAN THAT BEAT HER?
PROBABLY BECAUSE HE ACTED LIKE TEENIE WAS HIS. DIDN'T EVEN BAT AN EYE.
AND THAT EXCUSES WHAT HE DID TO HELEN?
AROUND HERE IT DOES. HE TREATED THAT GIRL LIKE SHE WAS BLOOD.
SOMETIMES MEN DO THE RIGHT THING, EVEN DRUNK ASSHOLES LIKE JAY.

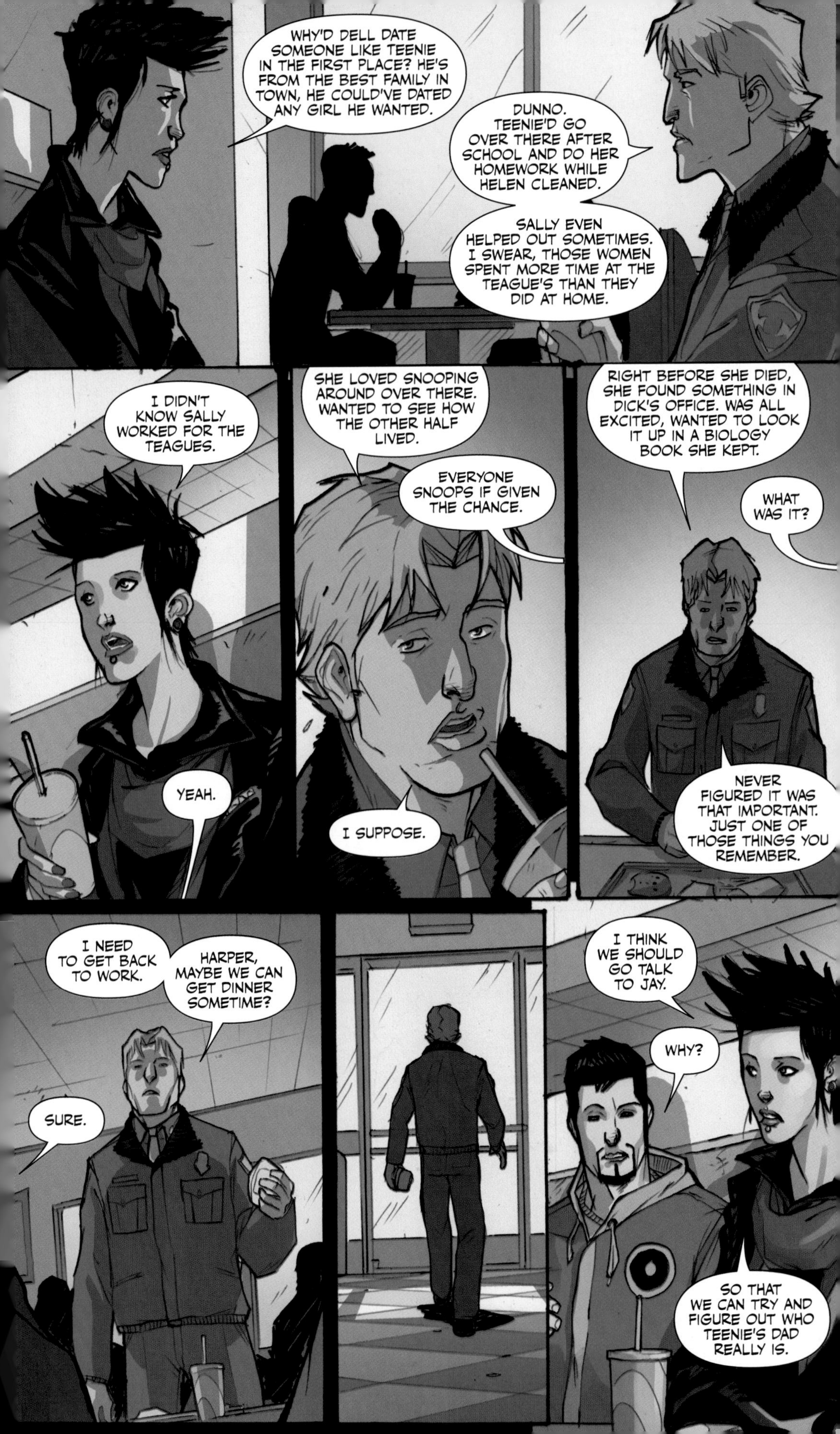
WHY'D DELL DATE SOMEONE LIKE TEENIE IN THE FIRST PLACE? HE'S FROM THE BEST FAMILY IN TOWN, HE COULD'VE DATED ANY GIRL HE WANTED.
DUNNO. TEENIE'D GO OVER THERE AFTER SCHOOL AND DO HER HOMEWORK WHILE HELEN CLEANED.
SALLY EVEN HELPED OUT SOMETIMES. I SWEAR, THOSE WOMEN SPENT MORE TIME AT THE TEAGUE'S THAN THEY DID AT HOME.
I DIDN'T KNOW SALLY WORKED FOR THE TEAGUES.
YEAH.
SHE LOVED SNOOPING AROUND OVER THERE. WANTED TO SEE HOW THE OTHER HALF LIVED.
EVERYONE SNOOPS IF GIVEN THE CHANCE.
I SUPPOSE.
RIGHT BEFORE SHE DIED, SHE FOUND SOMETHING IN DICK'S OFFICE. WAS ALL EXCITED, WANTED TO LOOK IT UP IN A BIOLOGY BOOK SHE KEPT.
WHAT WAS IT?
NEVER FIGURED IT WAS THAT IMPORTANT. JUST ONE OF THOSE THINGS YOU REMEMBER.
I NEED TO GET BACK TO WORK.
HARPER, MAYBE WE CAN GET DINNER SOMETIME?
SURE.
I THINK WE SHOULD GO TALK TO JAY.
WHY?
SO THAT WE CAN TRY AND FIGURE OUT WHO TEENIE'S DAD REALLY IS.

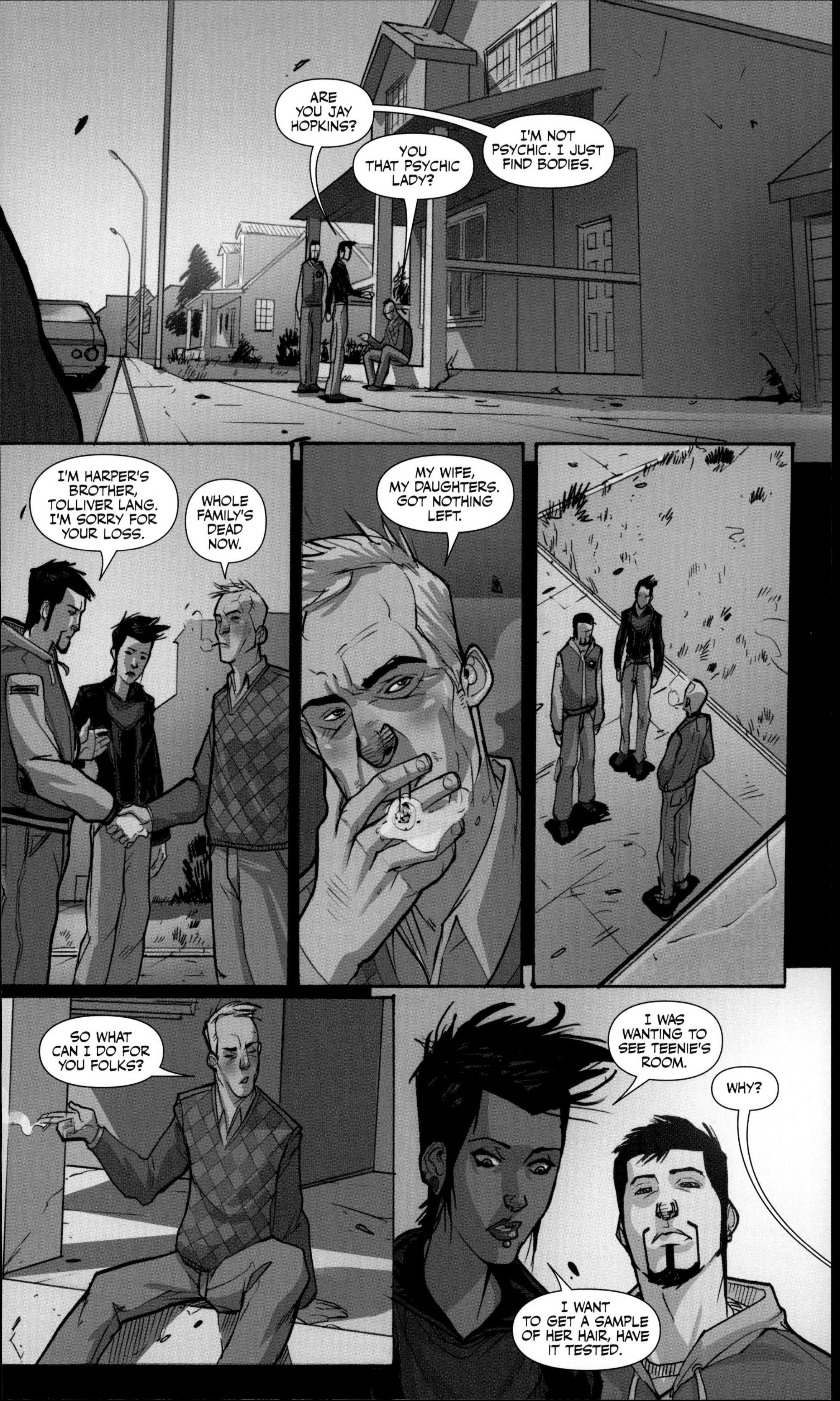

ARE YOU JAY HOPKINS?
I'M NOT PSYCHIC. I JUST FIND BODIES.
YOU THAT PSYCHIC LADY?
I'M HARPER'S BROTHER, TOLLIVER LANG. I'M SORRY FOR YOUR LOSS.
WHOLE FAMILY'S DEAD NOW.
MY WIFE, MY DAUGHTERS. GOT NOTHING LEFT.
SO WHAT CAN I DO FOR YOU FOLKS?
I WAS WANTING TO SEE TEENIE'S ROOM.
WHY?
I WANT TO GET A SAMPLE OF HER HAIR, HAVE IT TESTED.

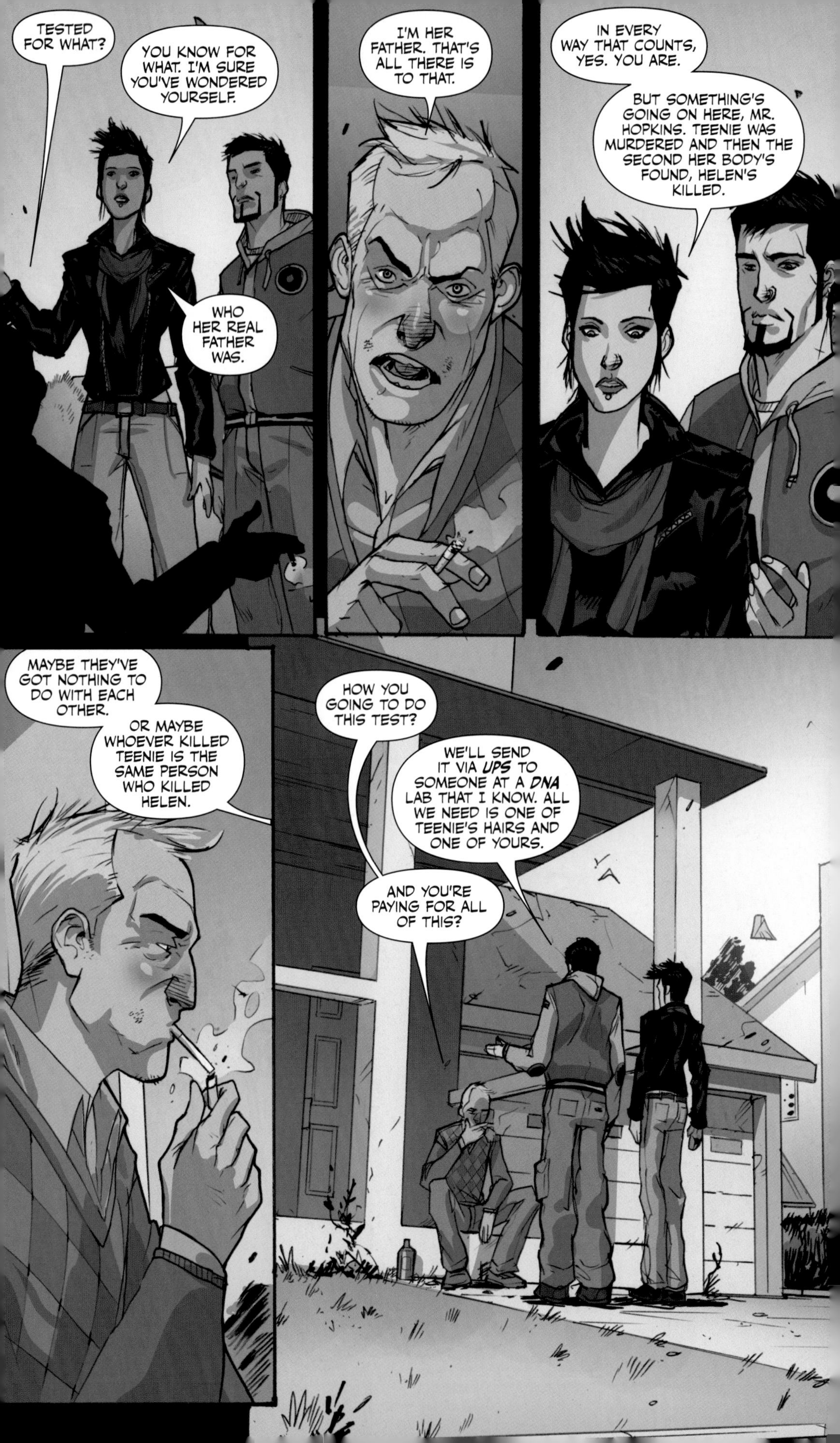
TESTED FOR WHAT?
YOU KNOW FOR WHAT. I'M SURE YOU'VE WONDERED YOURSELF.
WHO HER REAL FATHER WAS.
I'M HER FATHER. THAT'S ALL THERE IS TO THAT.
IN EVERY WAY THAT COUNTS, YES. YOU ARE.
BUT SOMETHING'S GOING ON HERE, MR. HOPKINS. TEENIE WAS MURDERED AND THEN THE SECOND HER BODY'S FOUND, HELEN'S KILLED.
MAYBE THEY'VE GOT NOTHING TO DO WITH EACH OTHER.
OR MAYBE WHOEVER KILLED TEENIE IS THE SAME PERSON WHO KILLED HELEN.
HOW YOU GOING TO DO THIS TEST?
WE'LL SEND IT VIA UPS TO SOMEONE AT A DNA LAB THAT I KNOW. ALL WE NEED IS ONE OF TEENIE'S HAIRS AND ONE OF YOURS.
AND YOU'RE PAYING FOR ALL OF THIS?

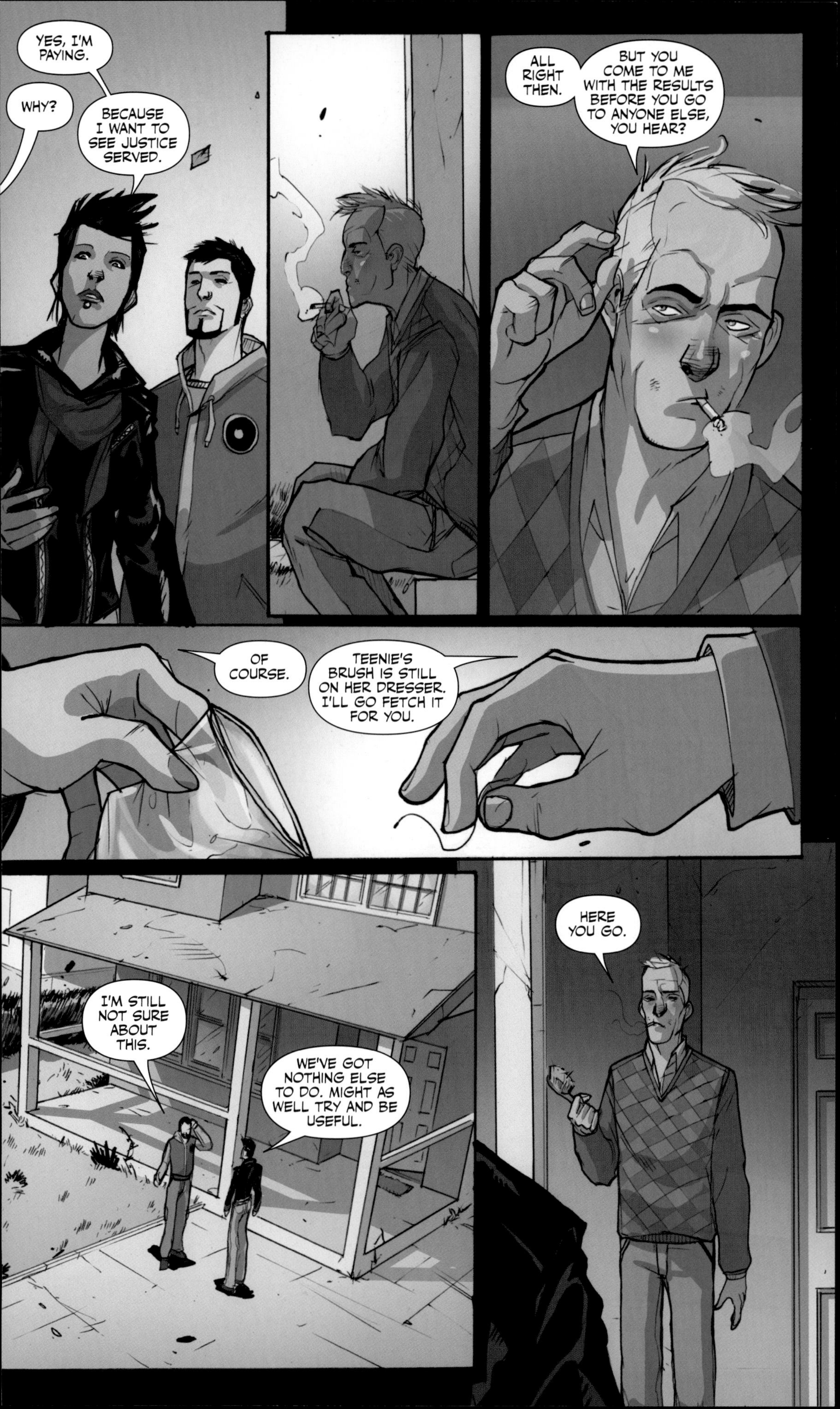

YES, I'M PAYING.
WHY?
BECAUSE I WANT TO SEE JUSTICE SERVED.
ALL RIGHT THEN.
BUT YOU COME TO ME WITH THE RESULTS BEFORE YOU GO TO ANYONE ELSE, YOU HEAR?
OF COURSE.
TEENIE'S BRUSH IS STILL ON HER DRESSER. I'LL GO FETCH IT FOR YOU.
I'M STILL NOT SURE ABOUT THIS.
WE'VE GOT NOTHING ELSE TO DO. MIGHT AS WELL TRY AND BE USEFUL.
HERE YOU GO.

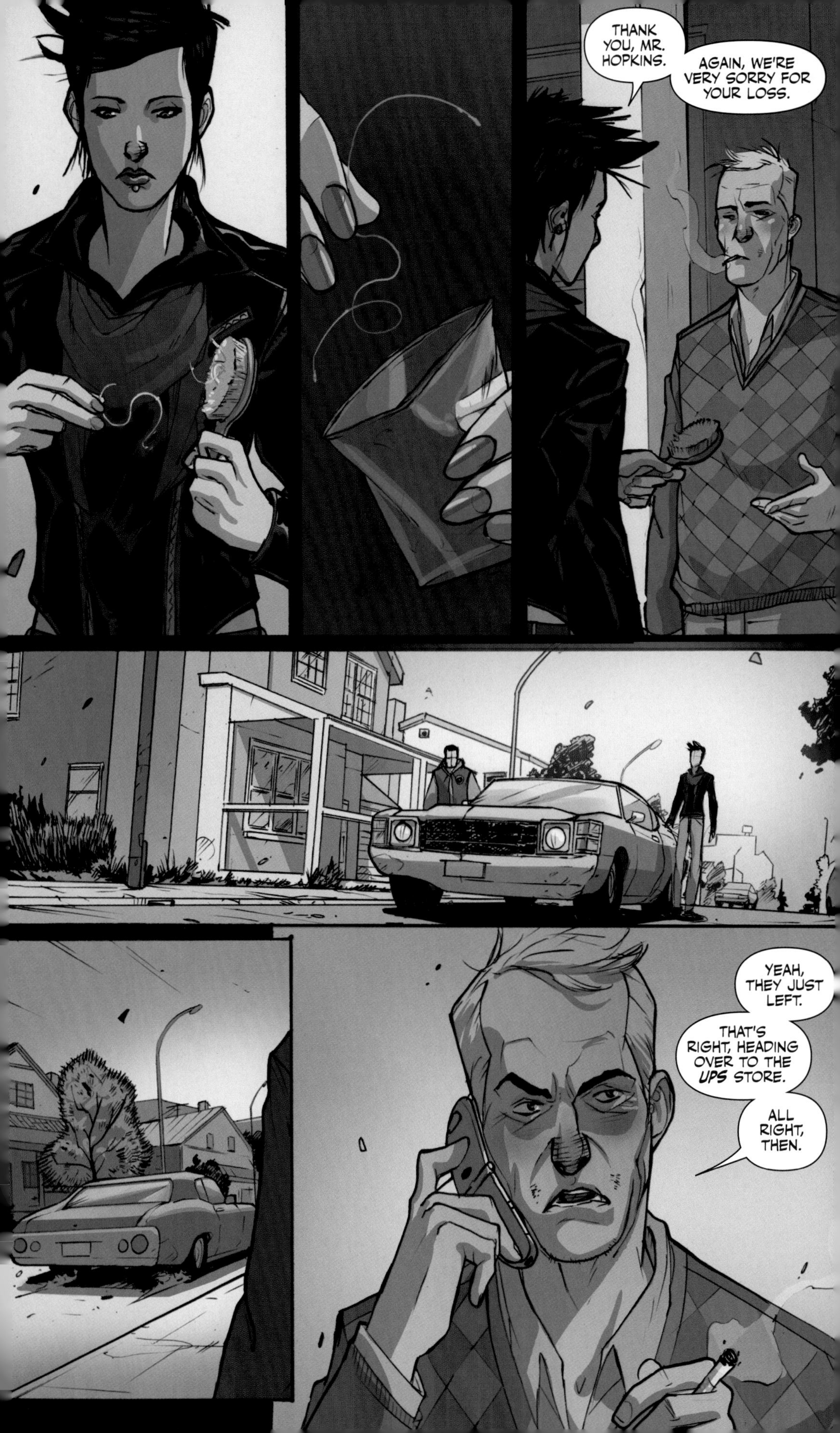
THANK YOU, MR. HOPKINS.
AGAIN, WE'RE VERY SORRY FOR YOUR LOSS.
YEAH, THEY JUST LEFT.
THAT'S RIGHT, HEADING OVER TO THE *UPS* STORE.
ALL RIGHT, THEN.

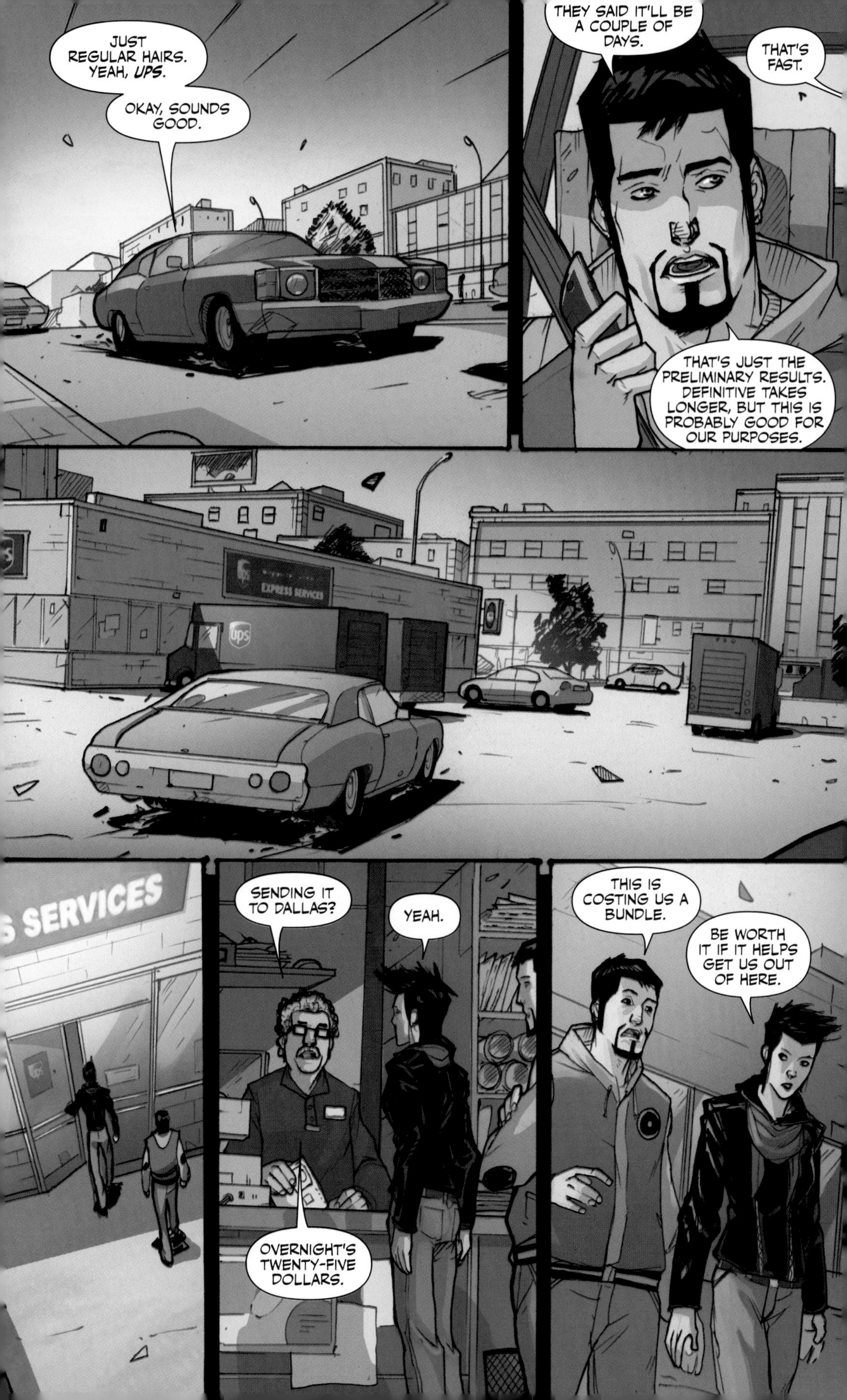
JUST REGULAR HAIRS. YEAH, UPS.
OKAY, SOUNDS GOOD.
THEY SAID IT'LL BE A COUPLE OF DAYS.
THAT'S FAST.
THAT'S JUST THE PRELIMINARY RESULTS. DEFINITIVE TAKES LONGER, BUT THIS IS PROBABLY GOOD FOR OUR PURPOSES.
EXPRESS SERVICES
UPS
S SERVICES
SENDING IT TO DALLAS?
YEAH.
OVERNIGHT'S TWENTY-FIVE DOLLARS.
THIS IS COSTING US A BUNDLE.
BE WORTH IT IF IT HELPS GET US OUT OF HERE.

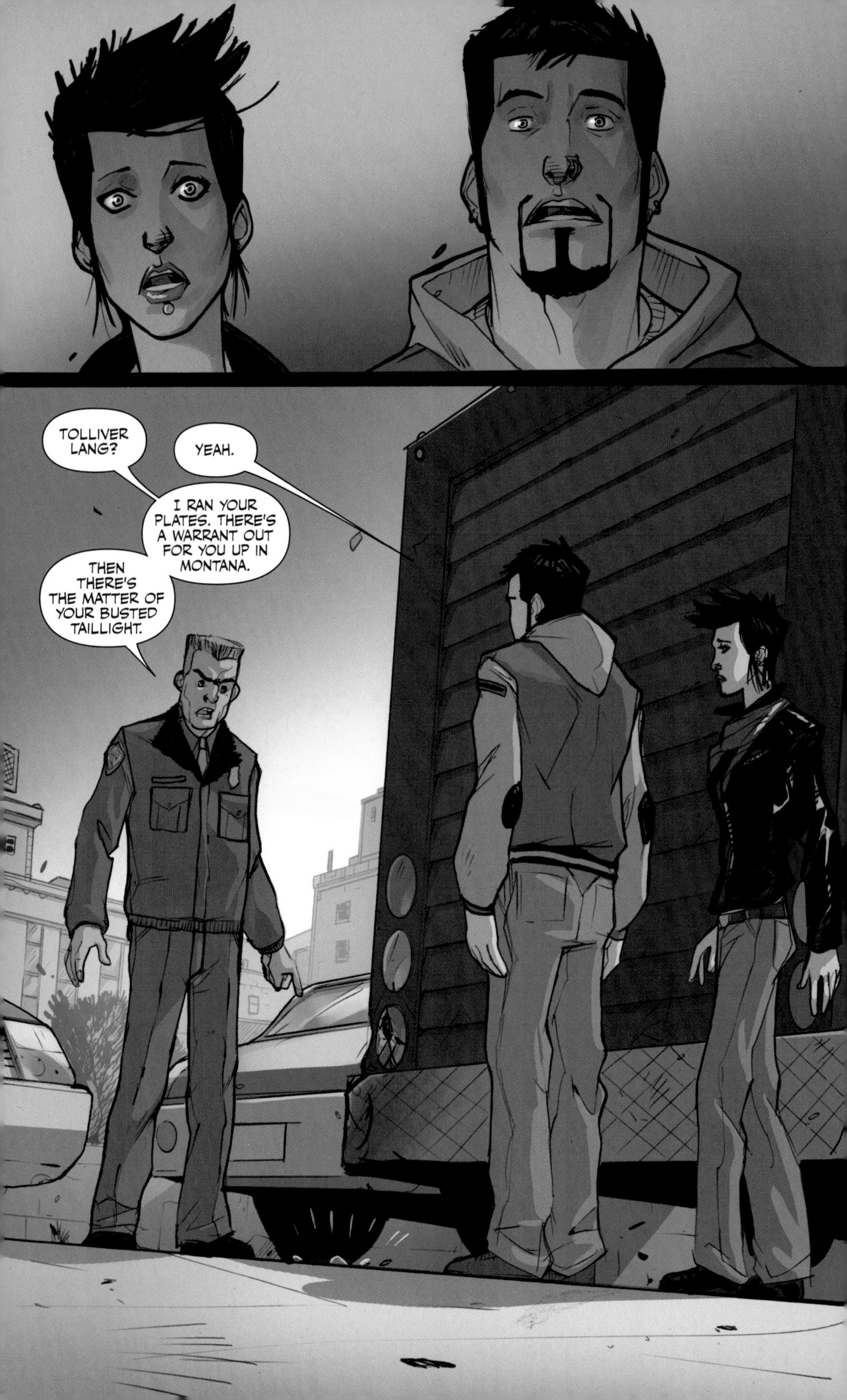
TOLLIVER LANG?
YEAH.
I RAN YOUR PLATES. THERE'S A WARRANT OUT FOR YOU UP IN MONTANA.
THEN THERE'S THE MATTER OF YOUR BUSTED TAILLIGHT.

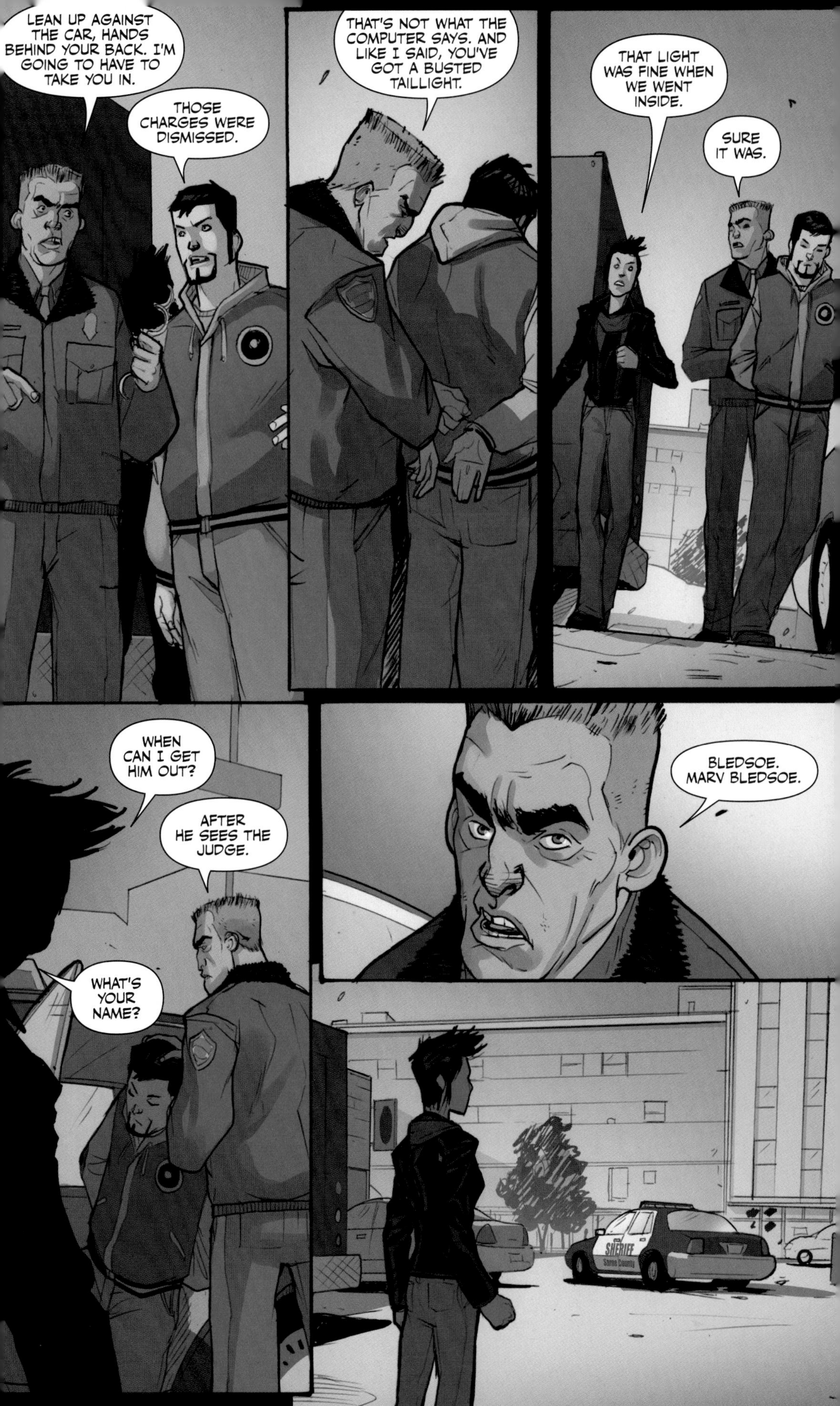
LEAN UP AGAINST THE CAR, HANDS BEHIND YOUR BACK. I'M GOING TO HAVE TO TAKE YOU IN.
THOSE CHARGES WERE DISMISSED.
THAT'S NOT WHAT THE COMPUTER SAYS. AND LIKE I SAID, YOU'VE GOT A BUSTED TAILLIGHT.
THAT LIGHT WAS FINE WHEN WE WENT INSIDE.
SURE IT WAS.
WHEN CAN I GET HIM OUT?
AFTER HE SEES THE JUDGE.
WHAT'S YOUR NAME?
BLEDSOE. MARV BLEDSOE.
SHERIFF

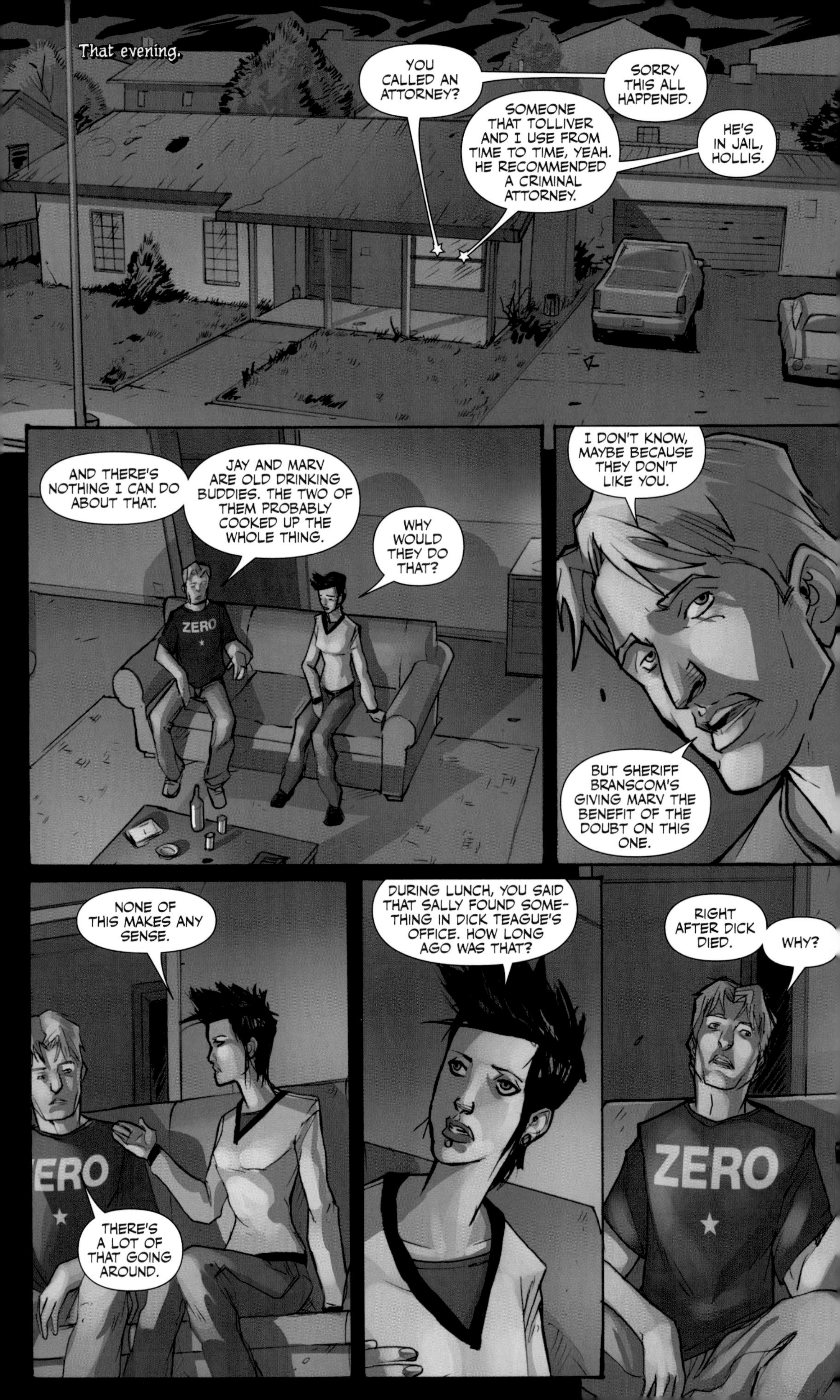
That evening.
YOU CALLED AN ATTORNEY?
SORRY THIS ALL HAPPENED.
SOMEONE THAT TOLLIVER AND I USE FROM TIME TO TIME, YEAH. HE RECOMMENDED A CRIMINAL ATTORNEY.
HE'S IN JAIL, HOLLIS.
AND THERE'S NOTHING I CAN DO ABOUT THAT.
JAY AND MARV ARE OLD DRINKING BUDDIES. THE TWO OF THEM PROBABLY COOKED UP THE WHOLE THING.
WHY WOULD THEY DO THAT?
ZERO
I DON'T KNOW, MAYBE BECAUSE THEY DON'T LIKE YOU.
BUT SHERIFF BRANSCOM'S GIVING MARV THE BENEFIT OF THE DOUBT ON THIS ONE.
NONE OF THIS MAKES ANY SENSE.
THERE'S A LOT OF THAT GOING AROUND.
DURING LUNCH, YOU SAID THAT SALLY FOUND SOMETHING IN DICK TEAGUE'S OFFICE. HOW LONG AGO WAS THAT?
RIGHT AFTER DICK DIED.
WHY?
ZERO

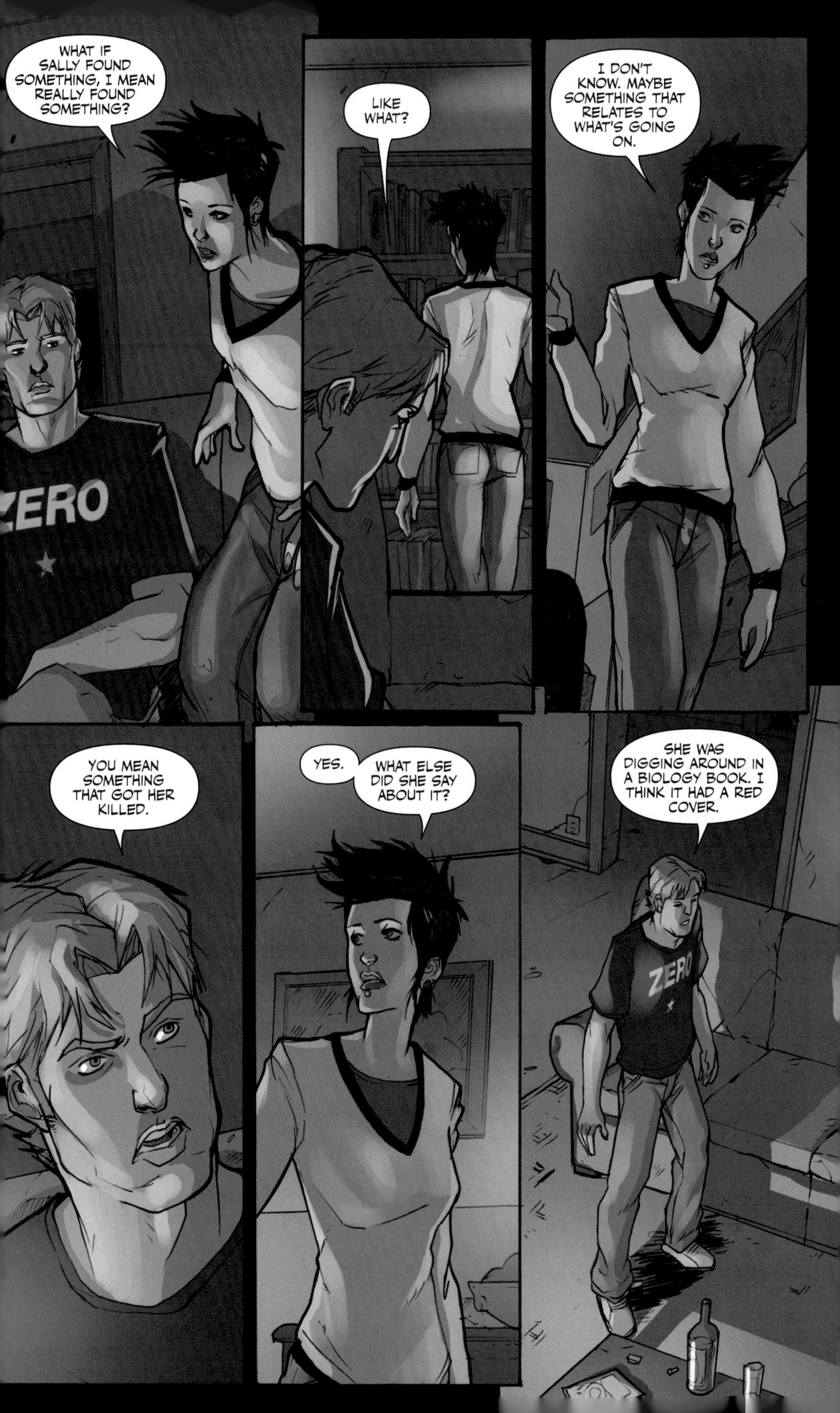
WHAT IF SALLY FOUND SOMETHING, I MEAN REALLY FOUND SOMETHING?
ZERO
LIKE WHAT?
I DON'T KNOW. MAYBE SOMETHING THAT RELATES TO WHAT'S GOING ON.
YOU MEAN SOMETHING THAT GOT HER KILLED.
YES.
WHAT ELSE DID SHE SAY ABOUT IT?
SHE WAS DIGGING AROUND IN A BIOLOGY BOOK. I THINK IT HAD A RED COVER.
ZERO

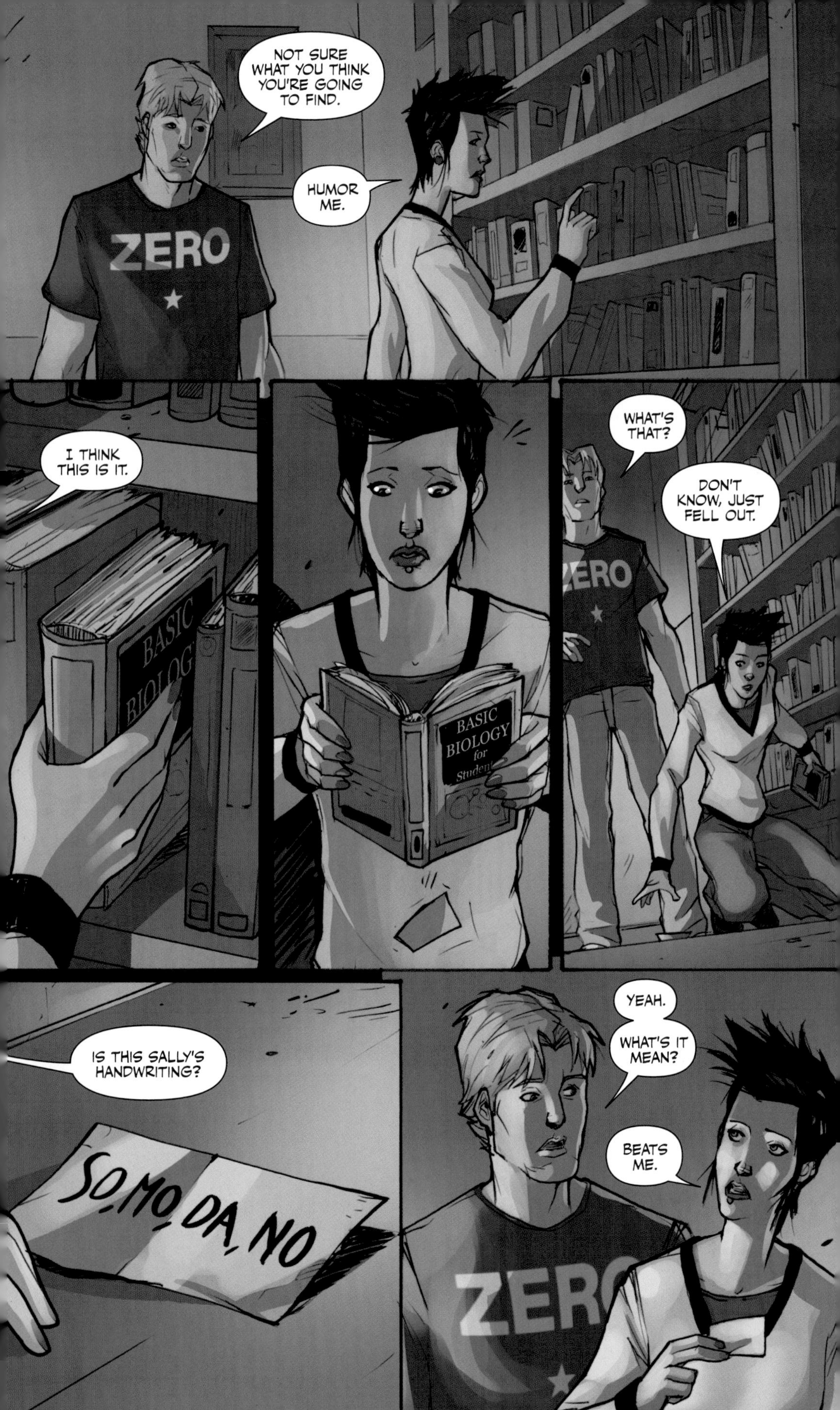
NOT SURE WHAT YOU THINK YOU'RE GOING TO FIND.
HUMOR ME.
ZERO
I THINK THIS IS IT.
BASIC BIOLOGY
BASIC BIOLOGY for Student
WHAT'S THAT?
DON'T KNOW, JUST FELL OUT.
IS THIS SALLY'S HANDWRITING?
SO MO DA NO
YEAH.
WHAT'S IT MEAN?
BEATS ME.

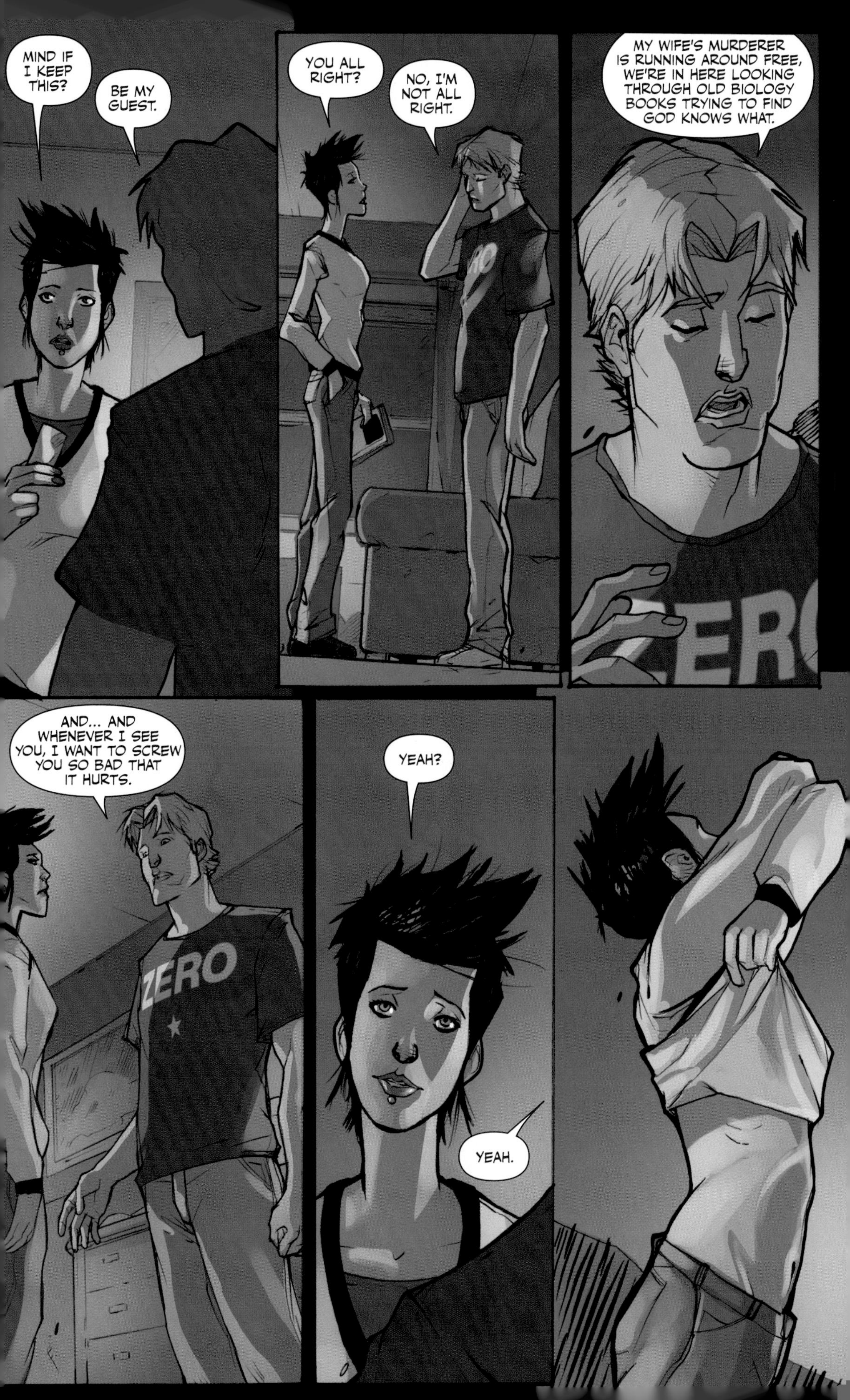
MIND IF I KEEP THIS?
BE MY GUEST.
YOU ALL RIGHT?
NO, I'M NOT ALL RIGHT.
MY WIFE'S MURDERER IS RUNNING AROUND FREE, WE'RE IN HERE LOOKING THROUGH OLD BIOLOGY BOOKS TRYING TO FIND GOD KNOWS WHAT.
AND... AND WHENEVER I SEE YOU, I WANT TO SCREW YOU SO BAD THAT IT HURTS.
YEAH?
YEAH.

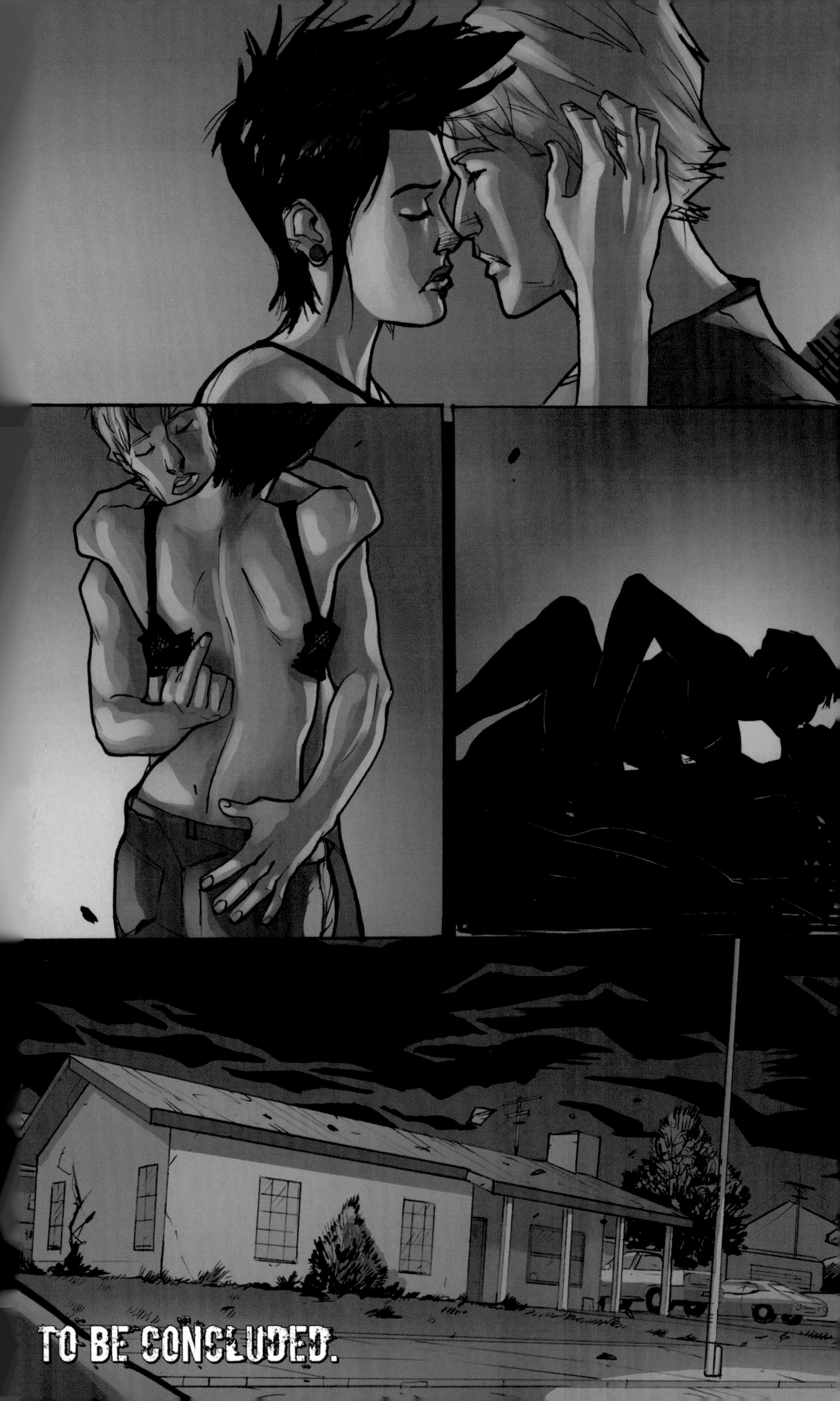
TO BE CONCLUDED.

GRAVE SIGHT
BONUS MATERIAL

THE MAKING OF GRAVE SIGHT

Letter From the Editor

Greetings!

Welcome to the bonus section of Grave Sight Part 2!

If you're reading this, chances are you picked up Part 1, and if so, we thank you! We hope you enjoy reading this as much as we've enjoyed putting it together...and that you find it's an interesting, yet faithful adaption of the novel.

As editor, it's my job to not only help pick the creative team, but also keep them on schedule, make sure everything is approved (in this case, by Charlaine), and that all makes sense at the end of the day.

For Grave Sight, we have assembled a fine, talented group, and they'll each be taking you through their creative process, and how they approached tackling this project in this bonus section, starting with writer Bill Harms, then to Mr. Denis Medri for the amazing artwork, on to Paolo Francescutto and his expressive colors, and finally to Bill Tortolini, for the often overlooked, but important task of lettering.

This project has been fun to work on, and I must say I'm quite proud of the work this team has produced. And I hope you agree!

We urge you to come back for the 3rd and final Part of Grave Sight, for the conclusion of the story, and an extended interview with Charlaine.

Until then...

Rich Young
Dynamite Entertainment

October 5, 2011

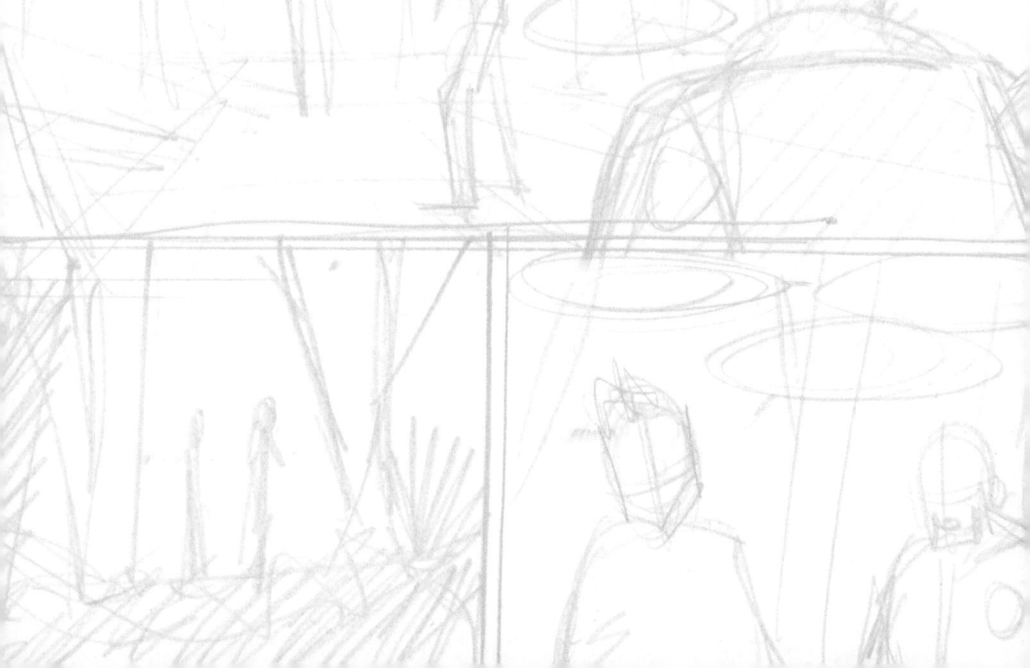

From Prose to Comic: Adapting Grave Sight
By William Harms

Comic books are unique in that they tell stories via a series of static images that, when paced properly, convey a sense of forward motion. There's an unspoken language between the creators and the reader that says if in one panel a character is reaching for a gun and in the next panel the character is firing that gun, the creators trusts the reader to mentally fill in the gap between the two actions.

So when I started work on adapting *Grave Sight*, I spent most of my time breaking the story down to its most vital parts and then arranging and constructing those parts so that they maintained the story that Charlaine told in the novel while also presenting that story in a visual way.

This was important because comic books are a visual medium where the art, not the writing, does the storytelling. (In fact, it's possible to tell wonderful stories with no words at all; Shaun Tan's *The Arrival* is a great example of this.) So although the oldest adage in writing is "show, don't tell", that is quite literally the way comic books are constructed. You start with the visuals and then layer everything else in.

So how do you take a novel like *Grave Sight* and reimagine it as a comic book? This is the process that I followed.

Reading and Deconstructing

After Rich Young asked me if I was interested in this project, I sat down and read *Grave Sight* two or three times. As I read it, I took a lot of notes that covered everything from important plot points to character descriptions, and even how the characters in the book knew each other.

Once all of my notes were assembled, I broke the story down into what are commonly called beats. These are usually one or two sentences that summarize a scene, and they're fairly easy to move around since the amount of text is small. Beats are a great way of quickly seeing whether the story is flowing properly, and if you're counter-balancing action scenes with quieter, character-focused scenes.

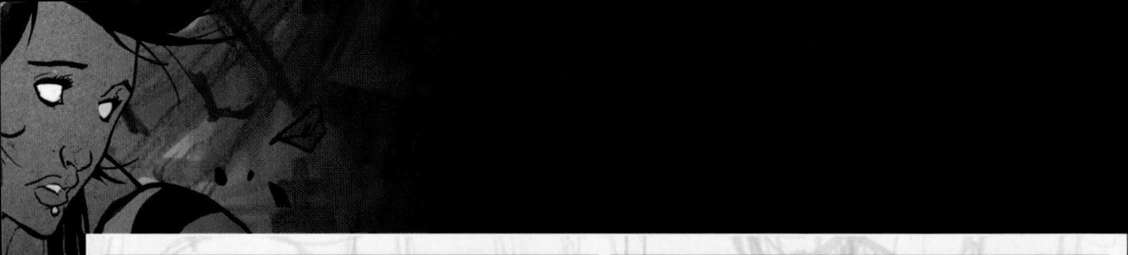

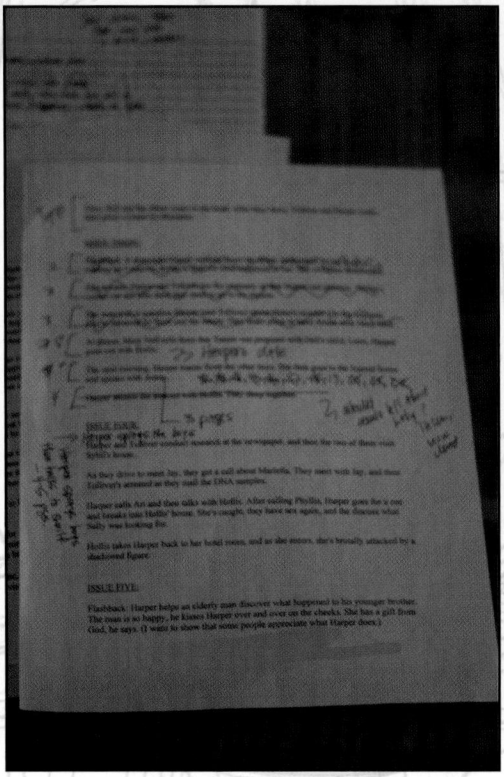

ISSUE FOUR

ISSUE FIVE

Flashback: Harper helps an elderly man discover what happened to his younger brother. The man is so happy, he kisses Harper over and over on the cheeks. She has a gift from God, he says. (I want to show that some people appreciate what Harper does.)

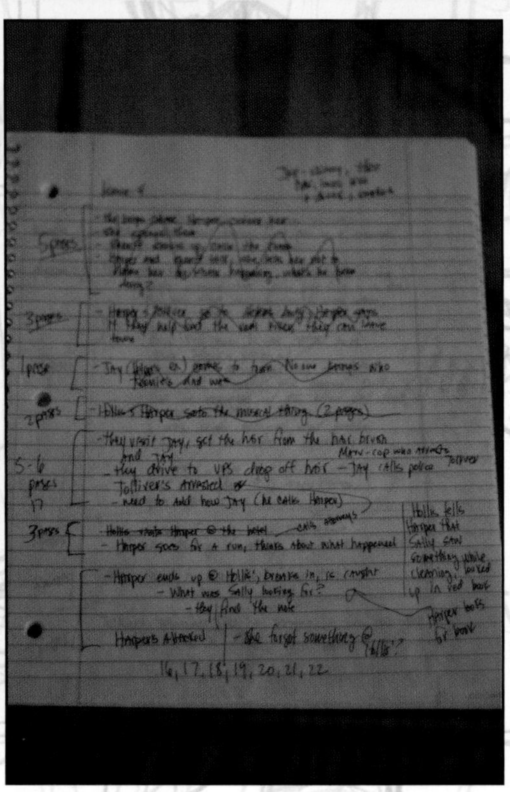

16, 17, 18, 19, 20, 21, 22

As I examined the beats, I realized a few things:

I wanted to open the first book with Tolliver's arrest in Montana. This incident comes up much later in the novel, but I wanted the comic to start with a burst of action that also quickly established the characters, specifically how most people view Harper and how loyal Tolliver is to her.

The disappearance of Cameron (Harper's sister) would play a more prominent role in the story. This was something I picked up on from the novel, and I simply expanded it, adding the idea that Harper always has a folder with information about Cameron's case, and that it pains Harper that she can't find her sister. It haunts her.

I wanted to add new scenes that show Harper using her powers in ways that people appreciated. This would not only help balance the opening scene in Montana, but it would also show that Harper, in her own unique way, was really helping people.

Finally, several scenes had to be condensed for space reasons. A great example of this is when Harper and Tolliver go out to look for Teenie's body — in the novel, Hollis is not with them. In the comic, he is. Simple things like this tightened the story so that it could fit within the confines of a comic book.

Scripts and Beats

I generally break down my comic scripts into 8-10 story beats (assuming the comic is 22 pages long), and I always try to end each issue with a cliffhanger and start the next one with something exciting. So before I started writing any of the scripts, I worked out the beats and then expanded or contracted each one depending on how many pages I thought each beat would need.

Although story beats act as sign posts that I need to follow to get where I need to go, that doesn't mean I'm not free to deviate from them. If a particular story thread suddenly feels more important than it did in the planning stages, it's important to follow where it goes.

With the beats worked out, I sat down and started scripting. It usually takes me a couple of days to write a complete comic script, but in this case it took longer because I'd have to constantly make decisions about narration and dialogue. Was I going to use dialogue from the book, or was I going to write new dialogue?

If it was the latter, I had to make sure that it matched the voice for each character that Charlaine created and didn't suddenly take the characters off in a direction that differed from the novel. At the start of the project, I generally wrote out Charlaine's dialogue and then I'd go back and edit it so that its length was more suitable for a comic book. Sometimes this meant no changes, sometimes it meant substantial changes.

Once the script was done, I'd usually sit on it for a day or two before I reread it and cleaned up any typos. Then it'd go off to Dynamite, who'd forward it to Charlaine and her agent. Once I incorporated their feedback, the script was finalized and it was sent off to Denis so that he could start on the art.

Throughout most of my writing career, I've generally focused on my own creations — such as *Impaler*, *Abel*, and *39 Minutes* — so taking someone else's work and adapting it was a pretty unique challenge. It exercised a completely different set of writing muscles, and in a lot of ways it was much harder than simply sitting down and writing my own story from scratch.

But in the end I'm really proud of the work Denis and I have done with this adaptation, and I hope that regardless of whether you're one of Charlaine's most devout readers — or someone who's never read the novel — that you find the story of Harper Connelly and her strange and wonderful gift entertaining and exciting.

From Script to Art: Illustrating Grave Sight

By Denis Medri

Here is a step-by-step look into the process that I use when working on my pages for *Grave Sight*. Step 1) I take the script and, after reading it, make a quick storyboard.

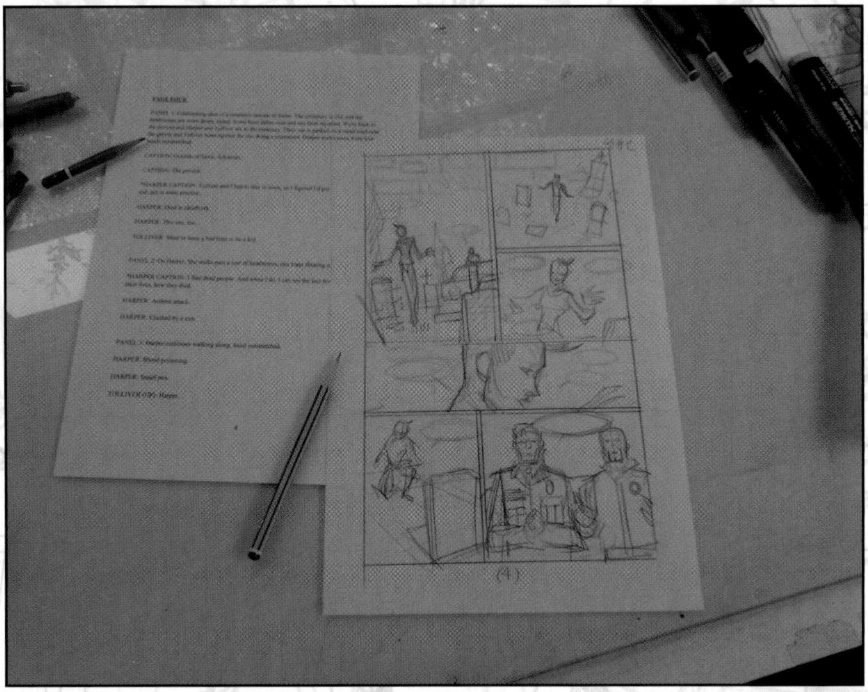

Step 2) Once the storyboards are approved, I do a layout on A3 format (sometimes fairly detailed, sometimes more simple). Here I "build" the sequences, expressions, poses, backgrounds, etc.

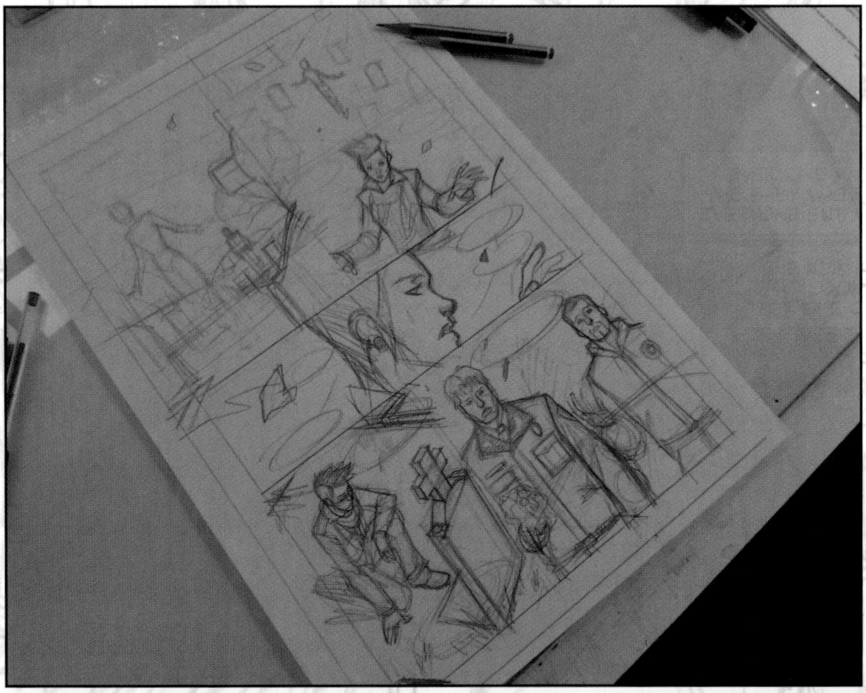

Step 3) Sometimes, but not always, I do a quick clean up of the panels before inking.

Step 4) Using a light box, I ink over my art and finish laying in all of the details with markers, pens, etc.

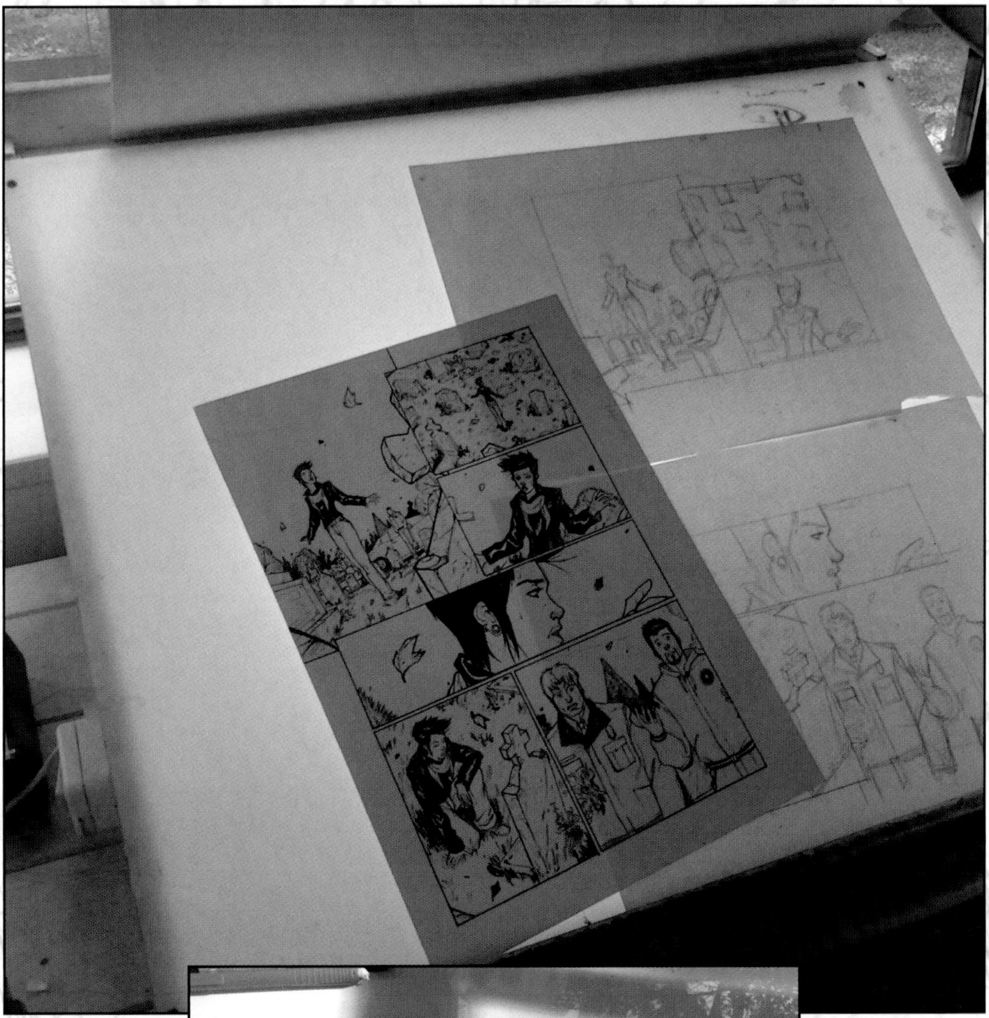

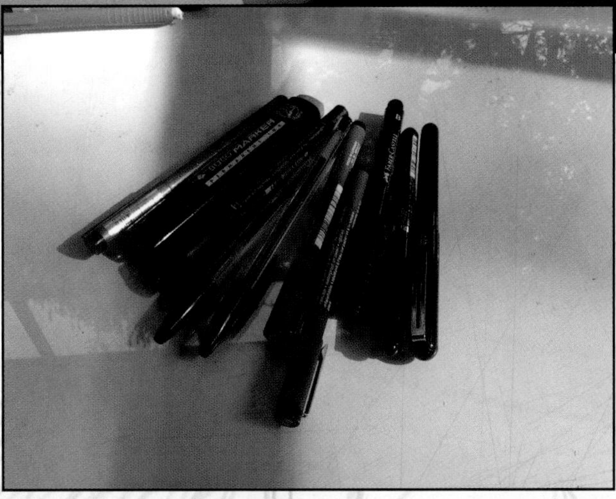

Step 5) I scan the page in high resolution, fixing any details that need to be fixed, and cleaning up anything that needs to be cleaned.

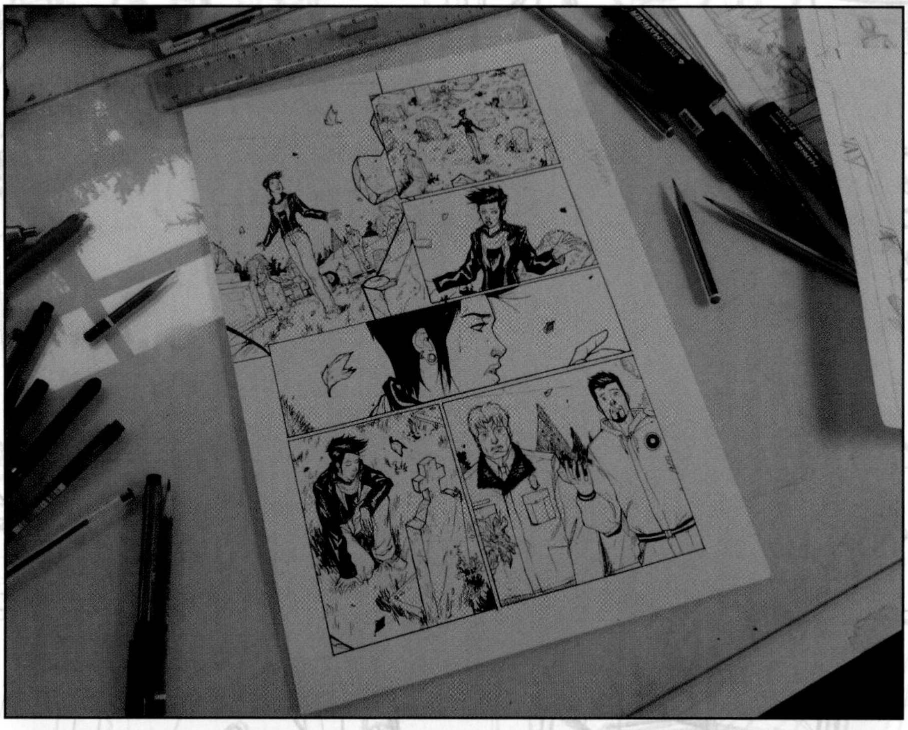

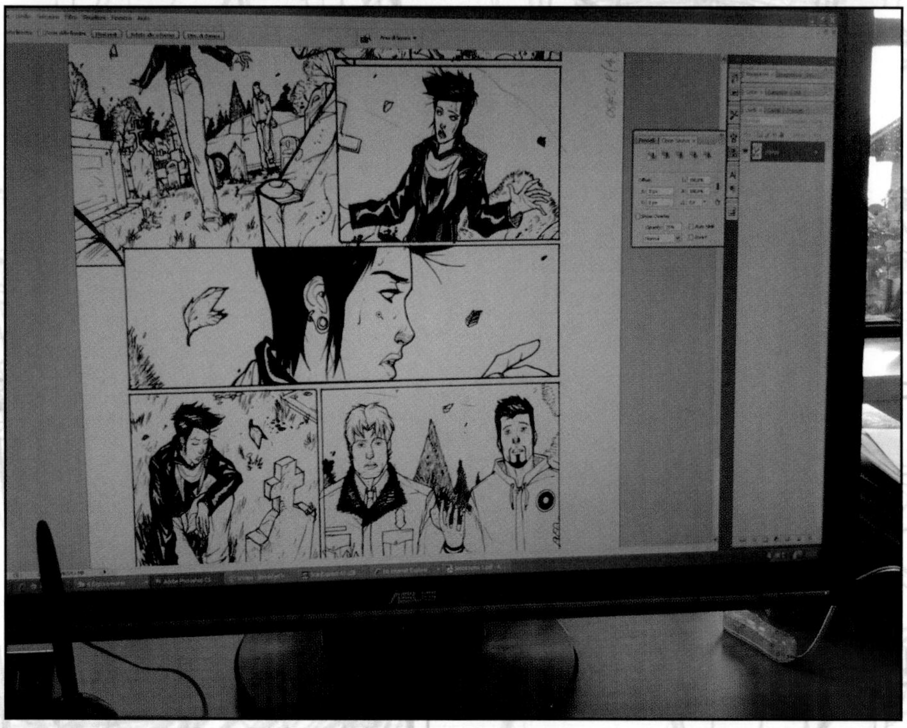

Step 6) With everything on my end complete, I upload the files to be colored and lettered.

From Art to Colors: Coloring Grave Sight
By Paolo Francesscutto

The following is a step-by-step guide from Paolo on how he goes about coloring pages, and specifically pages from this project, in Photoshop.*

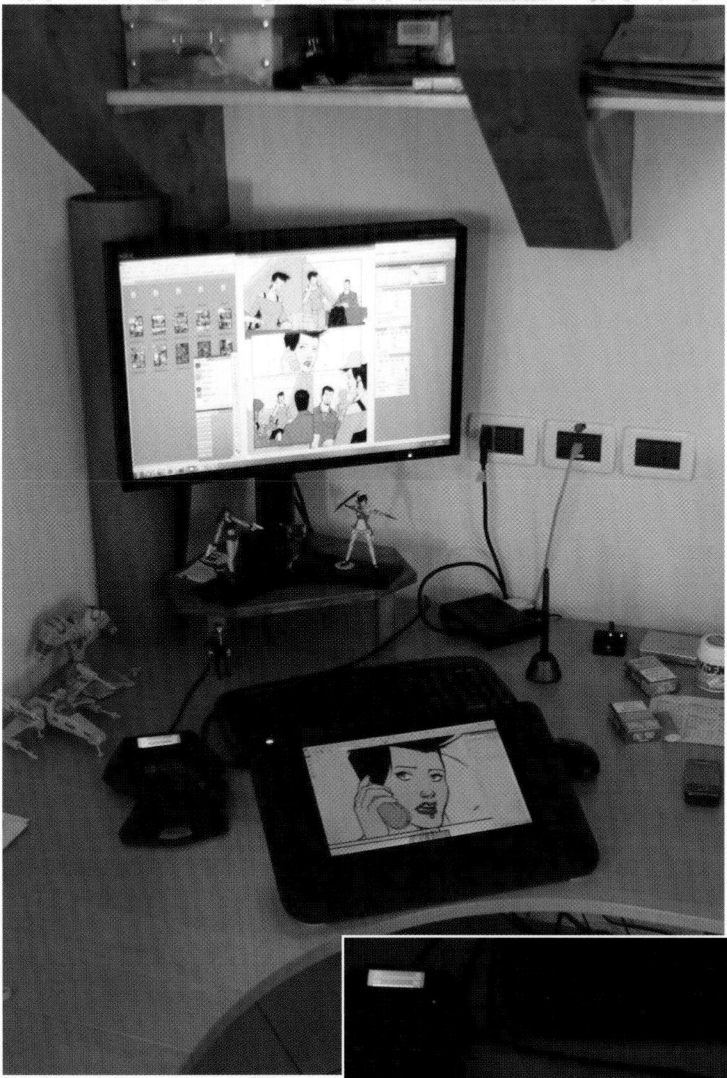

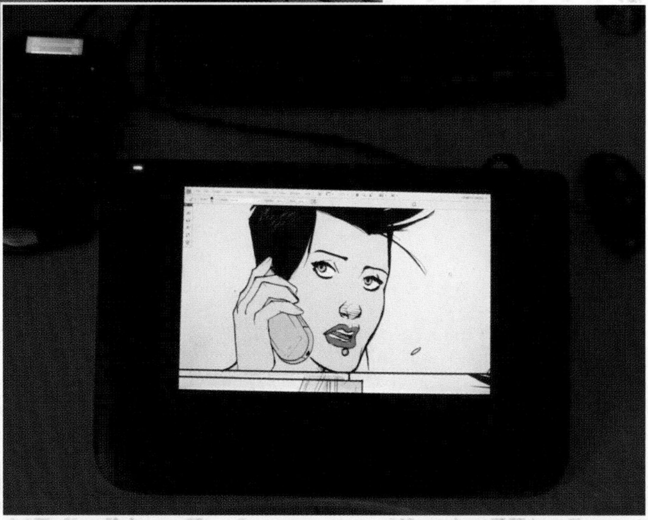

*Editor's Note: Since Paolo's native tongue is Italian, we have had to translate his words into English. Our apologies in advance for any mis-translations!

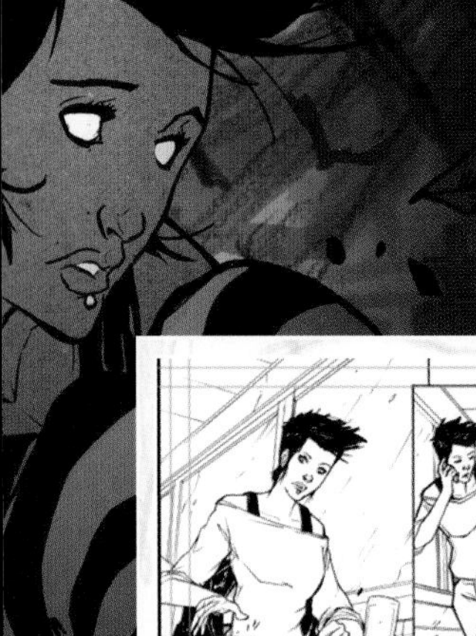

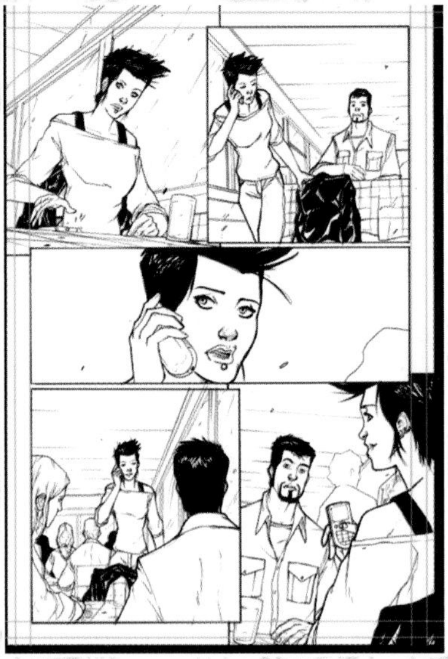

Step 1) The first step is to arrange the artist's inked art to fit the format required by the publisher.

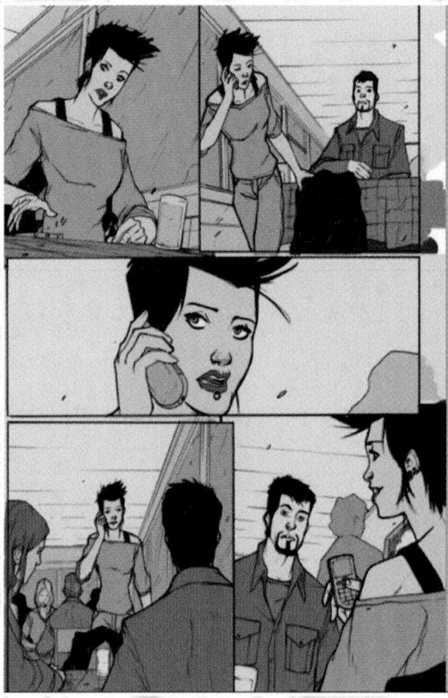

Step 2) Next I add the basic colors used across the page, this gives everything its own color reference.

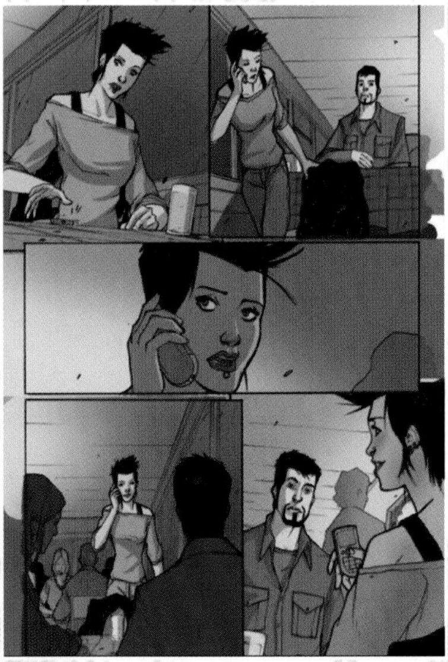

Step 3) Then I begin to fill in the shadows, depending on the needs and expression that the the setting requires.

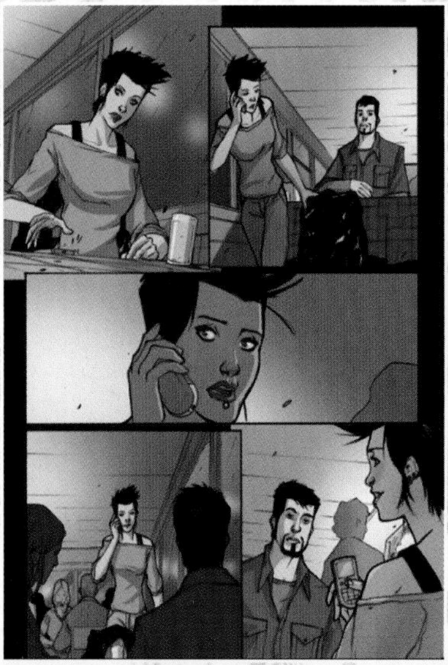

Step 4) Lighting and shading helps to emphasize emotions or actions. Lastly, I go back and make any corrections I feel must be made to finish the page.

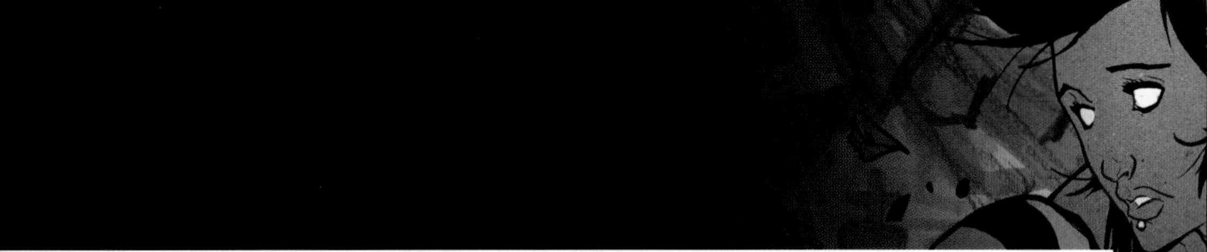

Last Stop on the Production Train: Lettering Grave Sight

By Bill Tortolini

Last man on the production train, that's the role of the letterist. We are the last set of hands to touch the story. We hand off our pages to the talented Graphic Designers who then prepare the book for press -- while adding their own additions to the design.

The process of lettering a comic seems simple. It's always the thought that the letterist will just open up a word processing program and type in the script and that's it. That is pretty far from the truth. Most letterers are trained graphic designers with years of experience under their belts. I am a 20 year graphic design vet. I graduated from college with honors in Art, and have studied typography for many years.

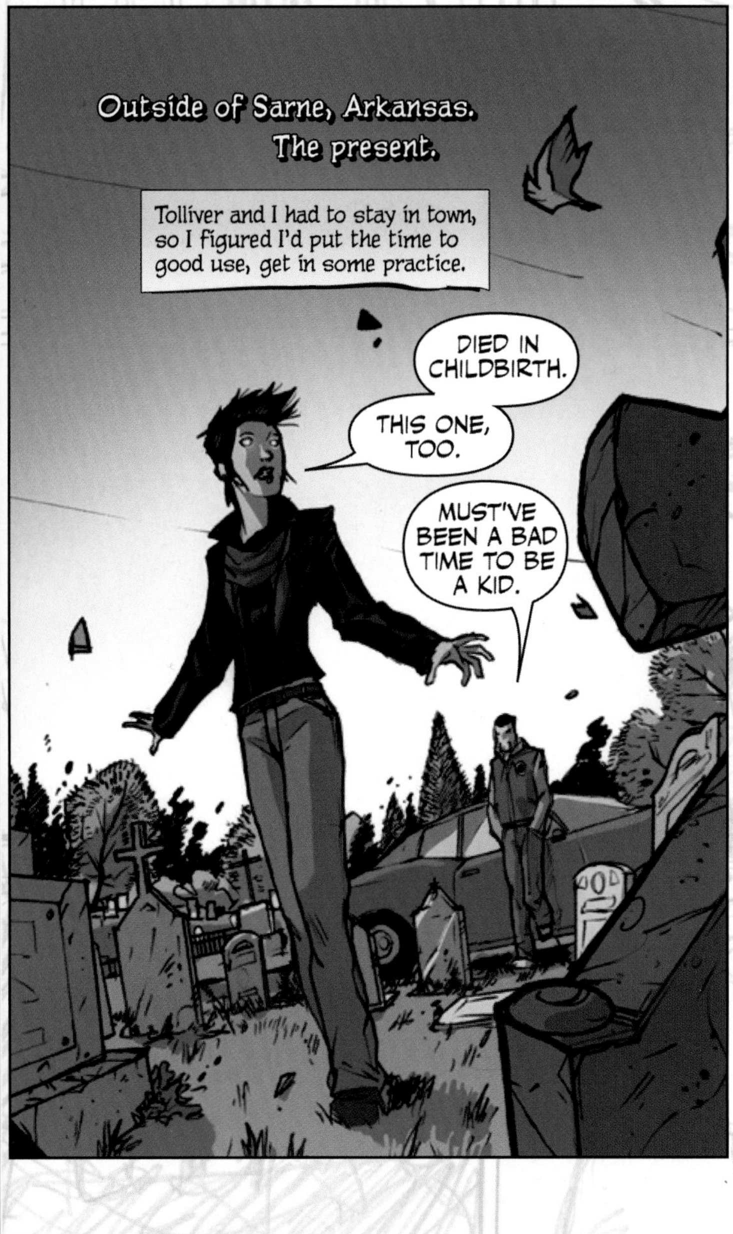

Outside of Sarne, Arkansas. The present.
Tolliver and I had to stay in town, so I figured I'd put the time to good use, get in some practice.
DIED IN CHILDBIRTH.
THIS ONE, TOO.
MUST'VE BEEN A BAD TIME TO BE A KID.

Grave Sight for me begins when the book is delivered to me to begin the process of lettering as soon as the artist finishes the first pass of the pages. My editor, Rich Young, delivers me the script with any notes from the writer and sets me along to my deadline. Once I get the pages I go through and look for any specific caption or dialogue cues that may need special treatment, and I design those elements. I then go through page by page working from the script and placing the dialogue pieces in a manner that helps continue to tell the story in a logical manner. As I reach the last page I export my files into a proper EPS file that I then deliver along to the production artist, where he'll place my final lettering file on top of the final color files. This process allows me to work at the same time as the colorist, cutting the production time a bit. After a review by the author, we go through our edits and send the final files off to print.

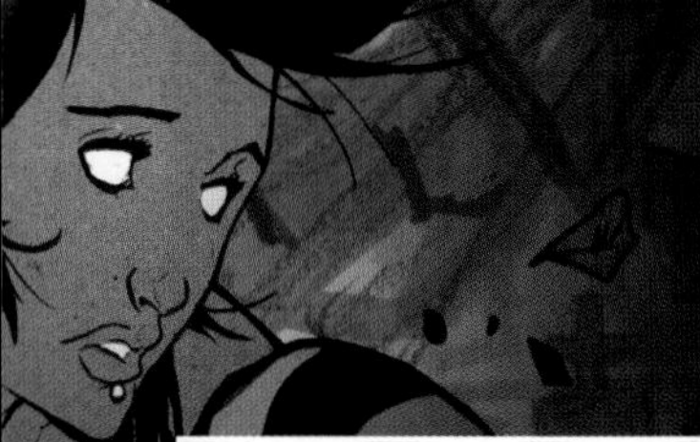

The font choices I made for *Grave Sight* reflect the soft edges and internal nature of our heroine. I've also muted the normal level of sound effects (or SFX in lettering lingo) with this book. In general I've gone through this project with the intention of not "scaring" away the non-traditional comic readers.

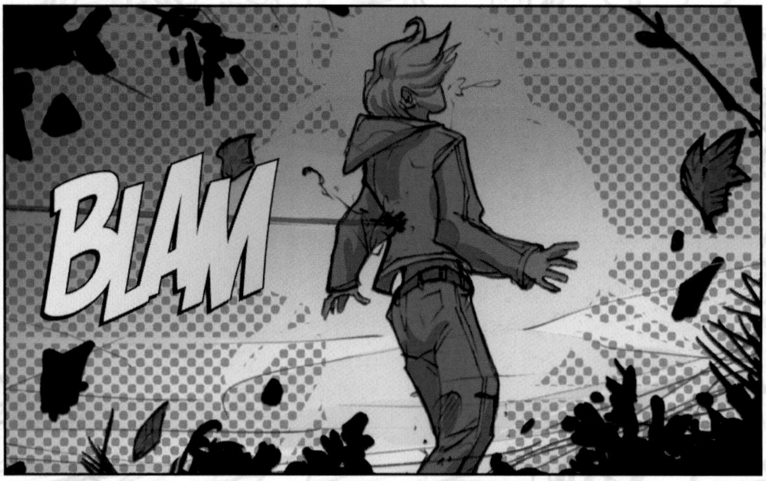
BLAM

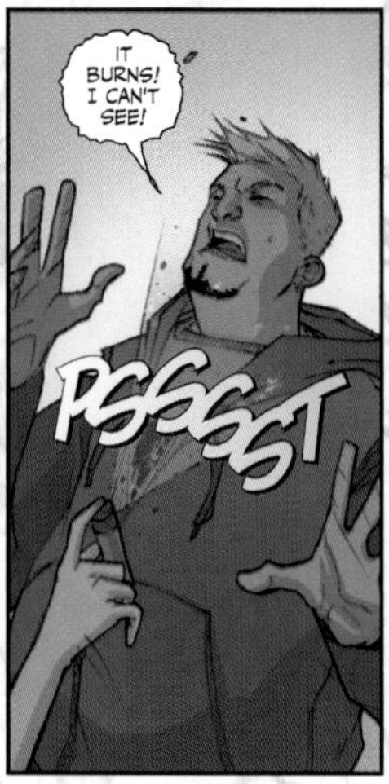
IT BURNS! I CAN'T SEE!
PSSSST

Lettering a book like *Grave Sight* is a pleasure. Such a strong story, with art work and story telling that is compelling on its own. My job is to lay the lettering down in such a way as to blend into the art, and keep the reader's eye moving in the proper direction. Keeping the untrained reader's eyes moving correctly from panel to panel is tough with books like Grave Sight, as this type of project does have a readership that may not be used to the left, right, top, down comic style.

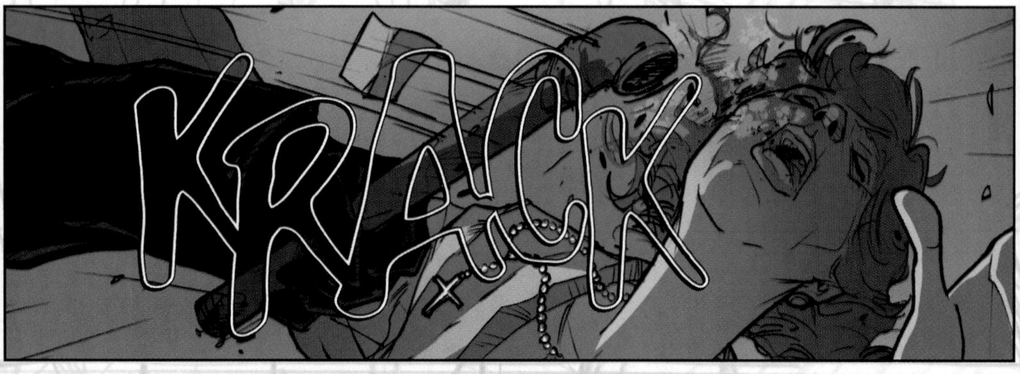
KRACK

The art of lettering a comic book is tough, because when lettering is done right, the reader never notices it. It's seamless. Done right, the reader is lead through a story without interrupting the flow of the story, without getting in the way of the art, and without pulling the reader back out into reality. But done wrong, lettering can be a distraction. It can ruin the hard work done by all the talented artists, inkers, colorists and writers. When done wrong, it is tragic.

Lettering may be the last part of comic design to be thought about, but without it - the story is silent.

GRAVE SIGHT FROM SCRIPT TO LETTERS

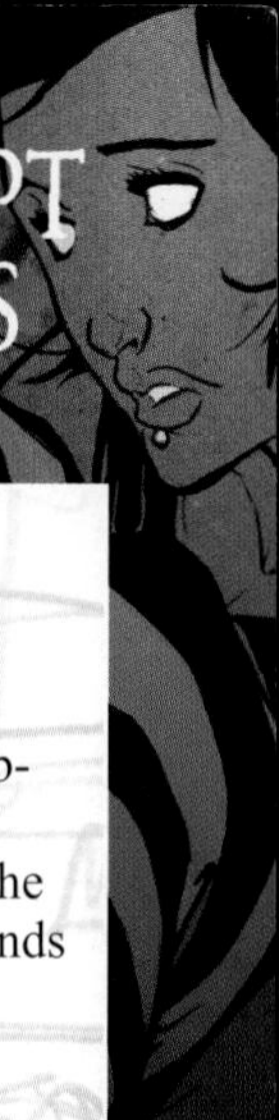

CHARLAINE HARRIS' GRAVE SIGHT # 2

PAGE FOUR

PANEL 1: Establishing shot of a cemetery outside of Sarne. The cemetery is old, and the tombstones are worn down, faded. Some have fallen over and not been repaired. We're back to the present and Harper and Tolliver are in the cemetery. Their car is parked on a small road near the graves and Tolliver leans against the car, doing a crossword. Harper walks away from him, hands outstretched.

CAPTION: Outside of Sarne, Arkansas.
CAPTION: The present.
*HARPER CAPTION: Tolliver and I had to stay in town, so I figured I'd put the time to good use, get in some practice.
HARPER: Died in childbirth.
HARPER: This one, too.
TOLLIVER: Must've been a bad time to be a kid.

PANEL 2: On Harper. She walks past a row of headstones, one hand floating over them.

*HARPER CAPTION: I find dead people. And when I do, I can see the last few moments of their lives, how they died.
HARPER: Asthma attack.
HARPER: Crushed by a tree.

PANEL 3: Harper continues walking along, hand outstretched.

HARPER: Blood poisoning.
HARPER: Small pox.
TOLLIVER (OP): Harper…

PANEL 4: Harper continues on.

HARPER (to Tolliver): Hang on.
HARPER: Flu.
HARPER: Pneumonia.

PANEL 5: Harper has stopped, looks down at an old tombstone.

HARPER: What do you know, this guy died from a gunshot wound.

PANEL 6: Standing next to Tolliver is Hollis. Tolliver gestures toward Hollis as if to say "I tried to warn you." Hollis holds a small bucket that's filled with weeds.

HOLLIS: That's Lieutenant Pleasant Early. He was killed during the Civil War.

PAGE FIVE

PANEL 1: Harper walks back to the car. Hollis stands by Tolliver.

HARPER: What are you doing here?
HOLLIS: Came out to weed my great-grandmother's grave.

PANEL 2: Tolliver looks in Hollis' direction. Tolliver's annoyed.

TOLLIVER: You have time to weed graves during murder investigations?

PANEL 3: Hollis looks at Tolliver. Hollis isn't used to people talking to him like this.

HOLLIS: It relaxes me.
HOLLIS: Besides, the state police took over this morning.

Top: rough layout by DENIS MEDRI
Center: final pencils and inks by DENIS MEDRI
Bottom: final colors by PAOLO FRANCESCUTTO
final letters by BILL TORTOLINI

Top: rough layout by DENIS MEDRI
Center: final pencils and inks by DENIS MEDRI
Bottom: final colors by PAOLO FRANCESCUTTO
final letters by BILL TORTOLINI

CREATOR IOGRAPHIES GRAVE SIGHT

CHARLAINE HARRIS

Charlaine Harris is a *New York Times* bestselling author who has been writing for thirty years. She was born and raised in the Mississippi River Delta area. She is also the author of the successful Sookie Stackhouse urban fantasy series about a telepathic waitress named Sookie Stackhouse who works in a bar in the fictional Northern Louisiana town of Bon Temps. Sookie Stackhouse has proven to be so popular that it has been adapted into *True Blood* for HBO. It was an instant success and is now filming its fourth season. Harris is married and the mother of three and lives in a small town in Southern Arkansas.

WILLIAM HARMS

William Harms has been a professional writer and editor for nearly 15 years. His comic book work has been published by Marvel Comics, DC Comics, Image Comics, and Top Cow, among others.

A finalist for the prestigious International Horror Guild Award -- one of the top literary awards for horror and dark fantasy -- William's comic and video game writing has received accolades from a wide variety of sources, including *The Daily Telegraph, USA Today, San Francisco Chronicle, Aint-it-Cool News, IGN Comics*, and *Fangoria*.

DENIS MEDRI

Denis Medri studied at the Institute of Arts in Forlì, graduated in 1998, and also attended the "Scuola del Fumetto" (School of Comics) of Milano. He has worked with various publishers in Italy, France and the USA including Les Humanoides Associès, Marvel Comics, Rainbow SPA, Image Comics, IDW Publishing, RCS/Gazzetta dello Sport, Panini, Vent d'Ouest and Dynamite Entertainment. He is primarily a comic artist, but also works as an illustrator, concept designer, caricaturist/portraitist, etc. His blog : http://denismedriartworks.blogspot.com

PAOLO FRANCESCUTTO

Paolo Francescutto is a founding parter of Gotem Studio, based in Friuli Veneziz Julia, in Italy. He has been a colorist, illustrator and comic book artist for the last 5 years, with clients in the French, Italian, and American markets, including Dynamite, Marvel, Soleils Productions, Glenat, and Del Court. While he colors on the computer, he also has a love for drawing in pencil, usually in a realistic style.

BILL TORTOLINI

Already an accomplished art director and graphic designer, Bill began lettering comics more than a decade ago and has worked with many of the comics industry's top creators and publishers.

Current and past projects include: *True Blood, Stephen King's Talisman, Anita Blake: Vampire Hunter, Army of Darkness, Random Acts of Violence, Wolverine, Back to Brooklyn, The Hedge Knight, Archie Comics, Riftwar, Battlestar Galactica, The Warriors, The Wheel of Time, The Dresden Files, Transformers, Star Trek: The Next Generation, G.I. Joe, The Last Resort*, and many others.

Bill is a graduate of Salem State University and resides in Billerica, Massachusetts with his wife and three children.

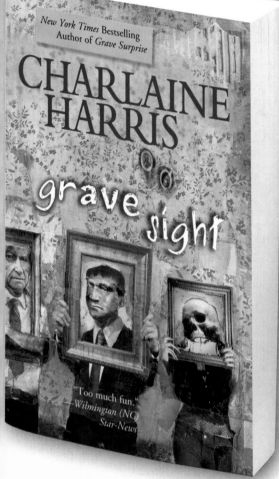

CURRENTLY AVAILABLE AND UPCOMING COLLECTIONS FROM DYNAMITE
For a complete list, visit us online at www.dynamite.net

ARMY OF DARKNESS:

Army of Darkness:
Movie Adaptation
Raimi, Raimi, Bolton

Army of Darkness:
Ashes to Ashes
Hartnell, Bradshaw

Army of Darkness:
Shop 'Till You Drop Dead
Kuhoric, Bradshaw, Greene

Army of Darkness vs.
Re-Animator
Kuhoric, Bradshaw, Greene

Army of Darkness:
Old School & More
Kuhoric, Sharpe

Army of Darkness: Ash vs.
The Classic Monsters
Kuhoric, Sharpe, Blanco

Army of Darkness:
From The Ashes
Kuhoric, Blanco

Army of Darkness:
The Long Road Home
Kuhoric, Raicht, Blanco

Army of Darkness:
Home Sweet Hell
Kuhoric, Raicht, Perez

Army of Darkness:
Hellbillies & Deadnecks
Kuhoric, Raicht, Cohn

Army of Darkness:
League of Light Assemble!
Raicht, Cohn

Army of Darkness
Omnibus Vol. 1
Hartnell, Kuhoric, Kirkman, more

Army of Darkness:
Ash Saves Obama
Serrano, Padilla

Army of Darkness vs. Xena
Vol. 1: Why Not?
Layman, Jerwa, Montenegro

Xena vs. Army of Darkness
Vol. 2: What...Again?!
Jerwa, Serrano, Montenegro

Darkman vs. Army of Darkness
Busiek, Stern, Fry

BATTLESTAR GALACTICA
New Battlestar Galactica Vol. 1
Pak, Raynor

New Battlestar Galactica Vol. 2
Pak, Raynor

New Battlestar Galactica Vol. 3
Pak, Raynor, Lau

New Battlestar Galactica
Complete Omnibus V1
Pak, Raynor, Jerwa, Lau

New Battlestar Galactica: Zarek
Jerwa, Batista

New Battlestar Galactica:
Season Zero Vol. 1
Jerwa, Herbert

New Battlestar Galactica:
Season Zero Vol. 2
Jerwa, Herbert

New Battlestar Galactica
Origins: Baltar
Fahey, Lau

New Battlestar Galactica
Origins: Adama
Napton, Lau

New Battlestar Galactica
Origins: Starbuck & Helo
Fahey, Lau

New Battlestar Galactica:
Ghosts
Jerwa, Lau

New Battlestar Galactica:
Cylon War
Ortega, Nylund, Raynor

New Battlestar Galactica:
The Final Five
Fahey, Reed, Raynor

Classic Battlestar Galactica
Vol. 1
Remender, Rafael

Classic Battlestar Galactica
Vol. 2: Cylon Apocalypse
Grillo-Marxuach, Rafael

GALACTICA 1980
Guggenheim, Razek

THE BOYS
The Boys Vol. 1
The Name of the Game
Ennis, Robertson

The Boys Vol. 2
Get Some
Ennis, Robertson, Snejbjerg

The Boys Vol. 3
Good For The Soul
Ennis, Robertson

The Boys Vol. 4
We Gotta Go Now
Ennis, Robertson

The Boys Vol. 5
Herogasm
Ennis, McCrea

The Boys Vol. 6
The Self-Preservation Society
Ennis, Robertson, Ezquerra

The Boys Vol. 7
The Innocents
Ennis, Robertson, Braun

The Boys Vol. 8
Highland Laddie
Ennis, McCrea

The Boys Vol. 9
The Big Ride
Ennis, Braun

The Boys
Definitive Edition Vol. 1
Ennis, Robertson

The Boys
Definitive Edition Vol. 2
Ennis, Robertson

The Boys
Definitive Edition Vol. 3
Ennis, Robertson, McCrea, more

THE GREEN HORNET
Kevin Smith's Green Hornet
Vol. 1 Sins of the Father
Smith, Hester, Lau

Kevin Smith's Green Hornet
Vol. 2 Wearing 'o the Green
Smith, Hester, Lau

Kevin Smith's Green Hornet
Vol. 3 Idols
Hester, Lau

Kevin Smith's Kato Vol. 1
Not My Father's Daughter
Parks, Garza, Bernard

Kevin Smith's Kato Vol. 2
Living in America
Parks, Bernard

Green Hornet: Blood Ties
Parks, Desjardins

The Green Hornet: Year One
Vol. 1 The Sting of Justice
Wagner, Campbell, Francavilla

The Green Hornet: Year One
Vol. 2 The Biggest of All Game
Wagner, Campbell

Kato Origins Vol. 1
Way of the Ninja
Nitz, Worley

Kato Origins Vol. 2
The Hellfire Club
Nitz, Worley

The Green Hornet: Parallel
Lives
Nitz, Raynor

The Green Hornet Golden Age
Re-Mastered
Various

THE LONE RANGER
The Lone Ranger Vol. 1:
Now & Forever
Matthews, Cariello, Cassaday

The Lone Ranger Vol. 2:
Lines Not Crossed
Matthews, Cariello, Cassaday, Pope

The Lone Ranger Vol. 3:
Scorched Earth
Matthews, Cariello, Cassaday

The Lone Ranger Vol. 4:
Resolve
Matthews, Cariello, Cassaday

The Lone Ranger & Tonto Vol 1
Matthews, Cariello, Guevara, more

The Lone Ranger Definitive
Edition Vol. 1
Matthews, Cariello, Cassaday

PROJECT SUPERPOWERS
Project Superpowers Chapter 1
Ross, Krueger, Paul, Sadowski

Project Superpowers Chapter 2
Vol. 1
Ross, Krueger, Salazar

Project Superpowers Chapter 2
Vol. 2
Ross, Krueger, Salazar

Project Superpowers: Meet The
Bad Guys
Ross, Casey, Lilly, Lau, Paul, Herbert

Black Terror Vol. 1
Ross, Krueger, Lilly

Black Terror Vol. 2
Ross, Hester, Lau

Black Terror Vol. 3
Inhuman Remains
Ross, Hester, Reis, Herbert

Death-Defying 'Devil Vol 1
Ross, Casey, Salazar

Masquerade Vol 1
Ross, Hester, Laul

RED SONJA
Adventures of Red Sonja Vol. 1
Thomas, Thorne, More

Adventures of Red Sonja Vol. 2
Thomas, Thorne, More

Adventures of Red Sonja Vol. 3
Thomas, Thorne, More

Red Sonja She-Devil With a
Sword Vol. 1
Oeming, Carey, Rubi

Red Sonja She-Devil With a
Sword Vol. 2: Arrowsmiths
Oeming, Rubi, more

Red Sonja She-Devil With a
Sword Vol. 3: The Rise of
Kulan Gath
Oeming, Rubi, more

Red Sonja She-Devil With a
Sword Vol. 4: Animals & More
Oeming, Homs, more

Red Sonja She-Devil With a
Sword Vol. 5: World On Fire
Oeming, Reed, Homs

Red Sonja She-Devil With a
Sword Vol. 6: Death
Marz, Ortega, Reed, more

Red Sonja She-Devil With a
Sword Vol. 7: Born Again
Reed, Geovani

Red Sonja She-Devil With a
Sword Vol. 8: Blood Dynasty
Reed, Geovani

Red Sonja She-Devil With a
Sword Vol. 9: War Season
Trautmann, Geovani, Berkenkotter

Red Sonja She-Devil With a
Sword Omnibus Vol. 1
Oeming, Carey, Rubi, more

Red Sonja vs. Thulsa Doom
Vol. 1
David, Lieberman, Conrad

Savage Red Sonja: Queen of
the Frozen Wastes
Cho, Murray, Homs

Red Sonja: Travels
Marz, Ortega, Thomas, more

Sword of Red Sonja: Doom
of the Gods (Red Sonja vs.
Thulsa Doom 2)
Lieberman, Antonio

Red Sonja: Wrath of the Gods
Lieberman, Geovani

Red Sonja: Revenge of the
Gods
Lieberman, Sampere

Savage Tales of Red Sonja
Marz, Gage, Ortega, more

VAMPIRELLA
Vampirella Masters Series Vol 1
Grant Morrison & Mark Millar
Morrison, Millar, more

Vampirella Masters Series Vol 2
Warren Ellis
Ellis, Conner Palmiotti, more

Vampirella Masters Series Vol 3
Mark Millar
Millar, Mayhew

Vampirella Masters Series Vol 4
Visionaries
Moore, Busiek, Loeb, more

Vampirella Masters Series Vol 5
Kurt Busiek
Busiek, Sniegoski, LaChanc, more

Vampirella Archives Vol 1
Various

Vampirella Archives Vol 2
Various

Vampirella Archives Vol 3
Various

Vampirella Archives Vol 3
Various

Vampirella Vol. 1
Crown of Worms
Trautman, Reis, Geovani

MORE FROM GARTH ENNIS
Dan Dare Omnibus
Ennis, Erskine

Garth Ennis' Battlefields
Vol. 1: The Night Witches
Ennis, Braun

Garth Ennis' Battlefields
Vol. 2: Dear Billy
Ennis, Snejbjerg

Garth Ennis' Battlefields
Vol. 3: The Tankies
Ennis, Ezquerra

Garth Ennis' The Complete
Battlefields Vol. 1
Ennis, Braun, Snejbjerg, Ezquerra

Garth Ennis' Battlefields
Vol. 4: Happy Valley
Ennis, Holden

Garth Ennis' Battlefields
Vol.5: The Firefly and His
Majesty
Ennis, Ezquerra

Garth Ennis' Battlefields
Vol.6: Motherland
Ennis, Braun

Garth Ennis' The Complete
Battlefields Vol. 2
Ennis, Braun, Holden, Ezquerra

Just A Pilgrim
Ennis, Ezquerra